PLANTS

by

LORRAINE CONWAY

illustrated by Linda Akins

cover design by Kathryn Hyndman

Copyright © Good Apple, Inc. 1980

ISBN No. 0-916456-69-2

Good Apple, Inc.
299 Jefferson Road
P.O. Box 480
Parsippany, NJ 07054-0480

Table of Contents

To the Teacher

PURPOSE: Active participation stimulates the processes by which learning takes place. It is with this thought in mind that the Good Apple Book of PLANTS was written. Basic concepts concerning plants come to life by means of labs, stations, packets, individual and group activities. The amount of time required for completion varies from a few minutes to an entire class period lending great variety in the use of the materials.

These activities were designed to require little or no expensive materials or elaborately equipped science rooms in order to arouse interest, stimulate curiosity and simplify basic biological truths.

MOBILE CLASSIFICATION OF PLANTS

PURPOSE: To use as an aid in the study of classification.

MATERIALS: Cardboard, poster or spray paint, dowels or coat hangers, string, and scissors.

PROCEDURE: Construct a mobile showing the steps in the classification of a plant. The first step on the mobile is the kingdom and the second phylum; then class, order, family, genus, and species may be used if desired. Use tags for names, outlines of the plants, or a combination of both. The mobile can be as simple or as detailed as you wish to make it; the important thing is to keep the steps in order.

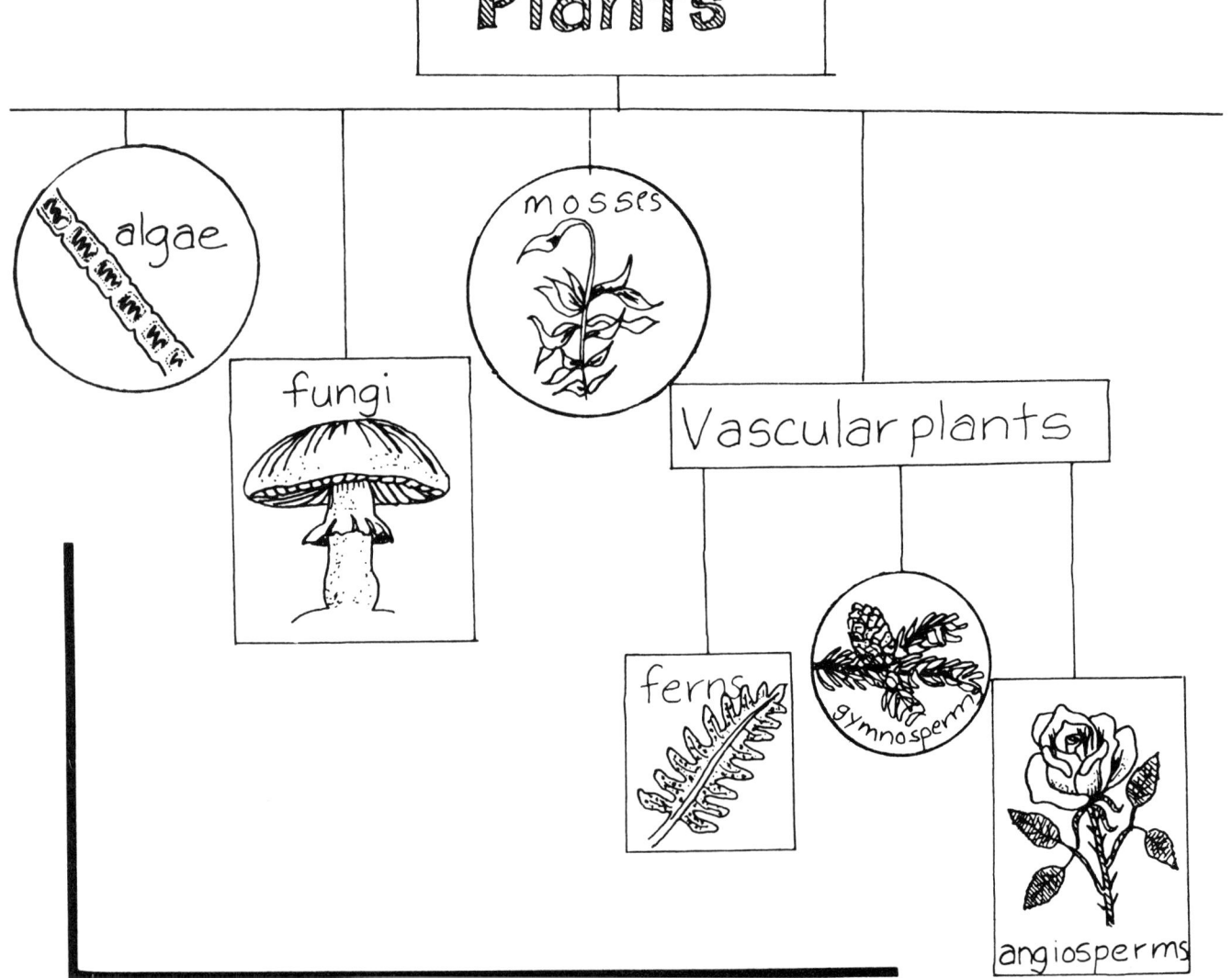

TREE STEM

PURPOSE: To learn the parts of a woody stem, to be able to tell the age of a tree by counting the annual rings.

MATERIALS: Slices of a tree. These can usually be obtained by asking the students to bring them in on a volunteer or extra-credit basis. Sometimes they can be obtained from a tree-cutter or a place where firewood is sold.

PROCEDURE: Have the students find on their tree stem slices as many parts shown on the diagram as possible. The questions on the sample sheet can be used for a study guide or discussion.

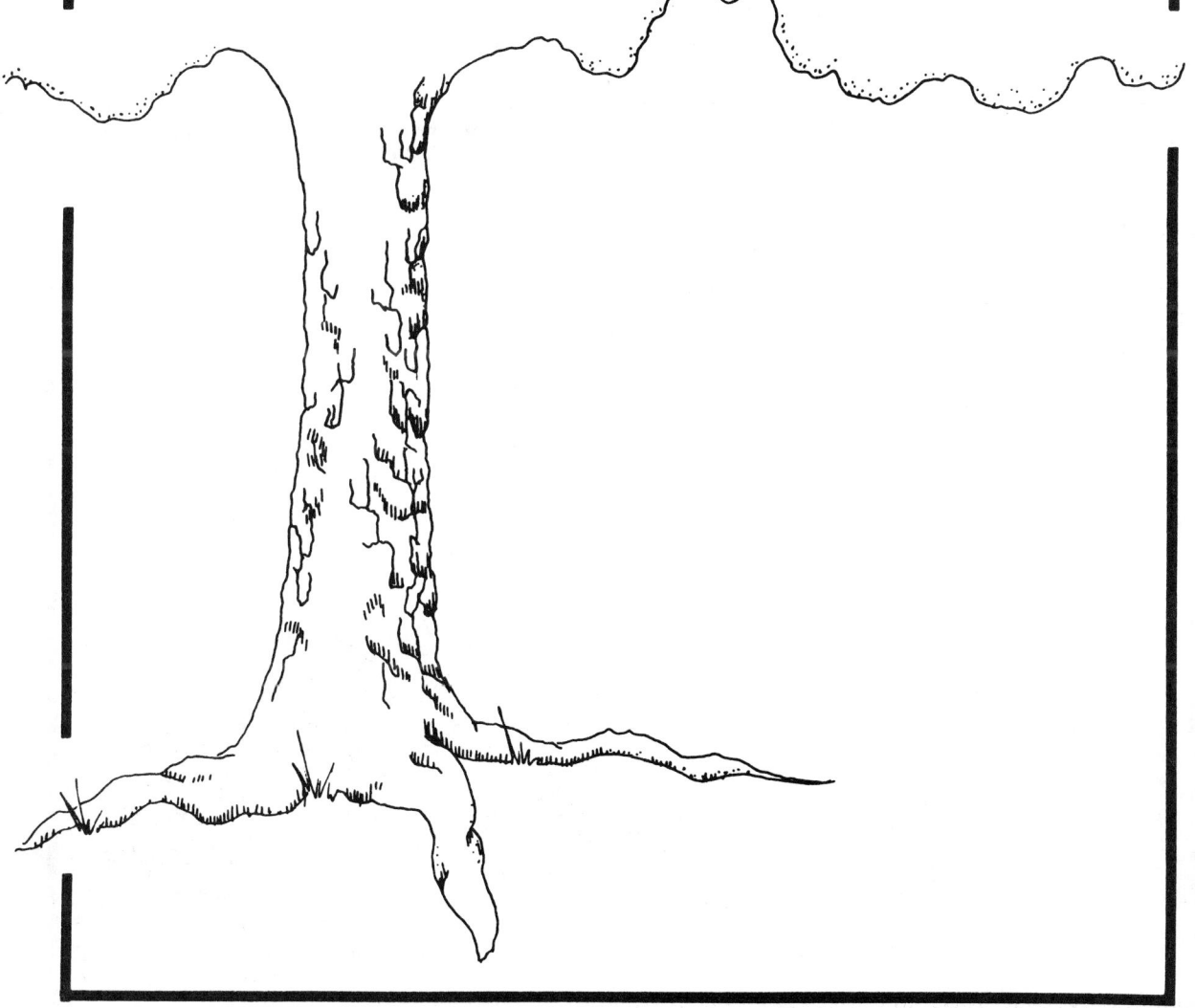

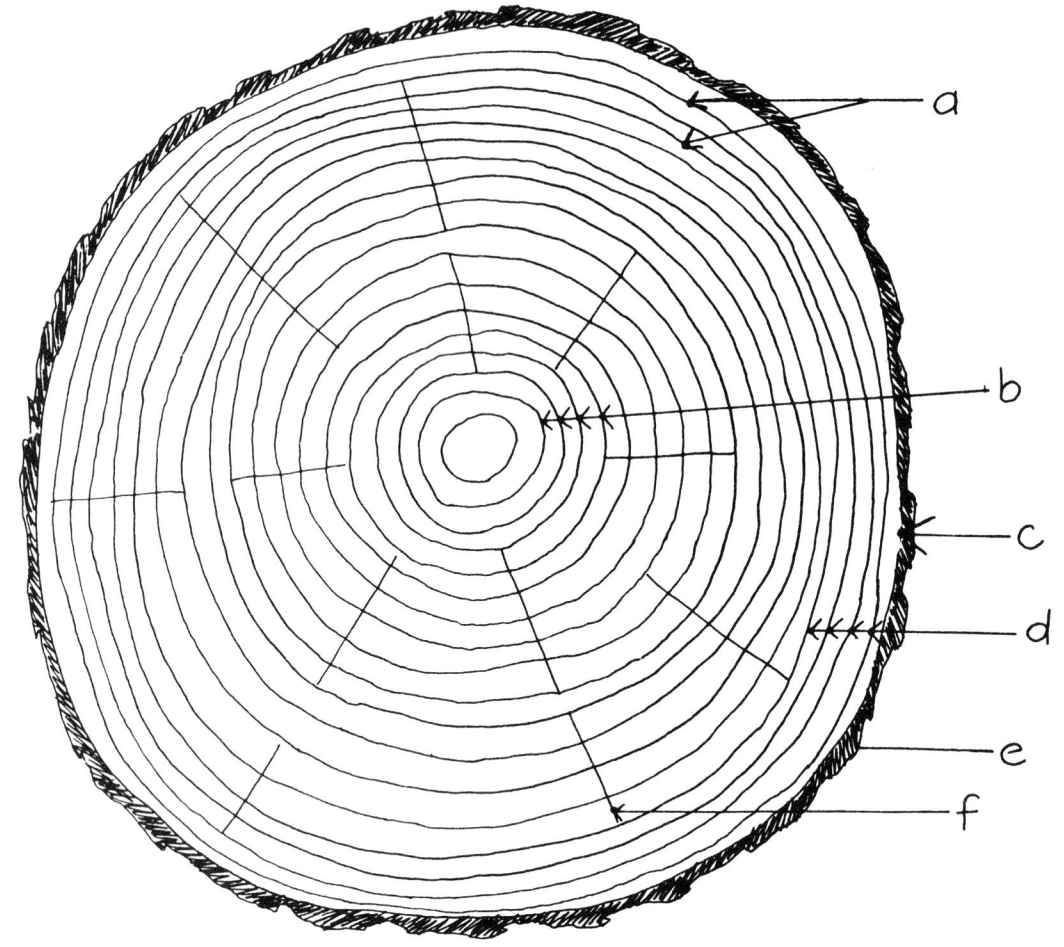

1. Identify the above parts on your tree stem. a. _____
   b. _____   c. _____   d. _____   e. _____
   _____   f. _____
2. How old is your tree? _____
3. If the above stem was cut in 1973, when was the tree planted? _____
4. Which is darker, the heartwood or the sapwood? _____
5. Which contains more moisture, the heartwood or the sapwood?
   _____
6. Which is more useful as lumber, heartwood or sapwood? _____
   _____
7. As the tree grows, which increases, the heartwood or the
   sapwood? _____
8. Which has more sapwood, an old tree or a young tree? _____
   _____
9. Is there any evidence of worm infestation in your tree
   sample? _____
10. Do you know what kind of tree your sample came from? _____
11. Does your sample tree have value as lumber? Why or why
    not? _____

THE STORY OF A TREE

PURPOSE: To enable the student to read the lines of a tree stem and gain knowledge of the life of a tree.

MATERIALS: A copy of the sample sheet and a pencil. This exercise can also be done with real tree slices. When the students have completed the copy sheet, they can write a story of their own tree stem.

PROCEDURE: Tell the story of the tree on the sample page, or write an original story from a real tree stem.

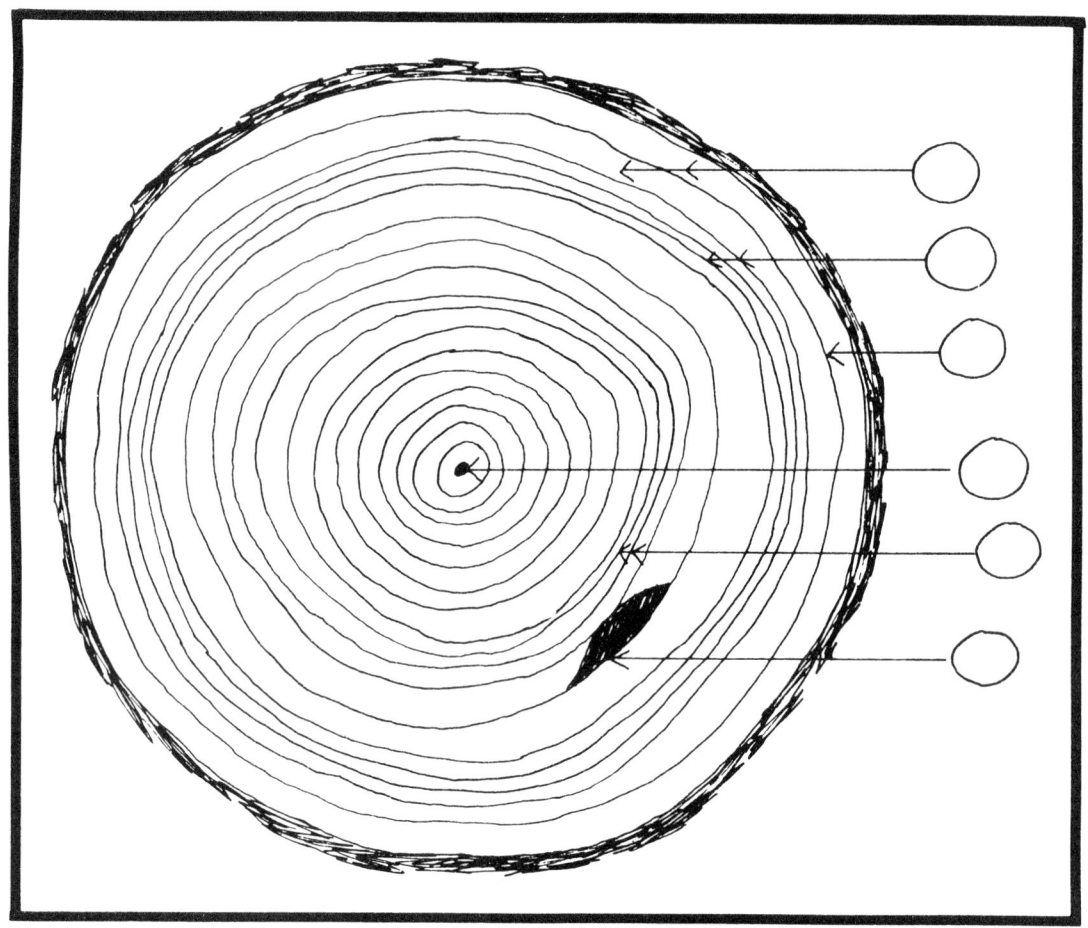

DIRECTIONS: If you correctly place the numbers in the above circles, you will tell the story of this little tree.

1. When this little tree was eight years old it began to lean because of an ice storm, and the rings are narrower on one side.
2. A seed fell to the ground, and this little tree was born.
3. A forest fire swept through, and this little tree was scarred.
4. These narrow rings were caused by a drought.
5. The large trees around this little tree were harvested, and this little tree is getting plenty of sunshine and water.
6. The little tree is now seventeen years old and growing well.

PARTS OF A FLOWER

PURPOSE: To learn the parts of a flower, to gain insight into plant reproduction.

MATERIALS: Specimens of various types of simple flowers to be brought in by the students. Roses, tulips, azaleas, petunias, etc., are very good for this exercise.

PROCEDURE: Give as many different kinds of flowers to each student or pairs of students as available. Locate the parts and answer the provided questions.

HINT: This exercise is best done in the spring when many flowers are easily available.

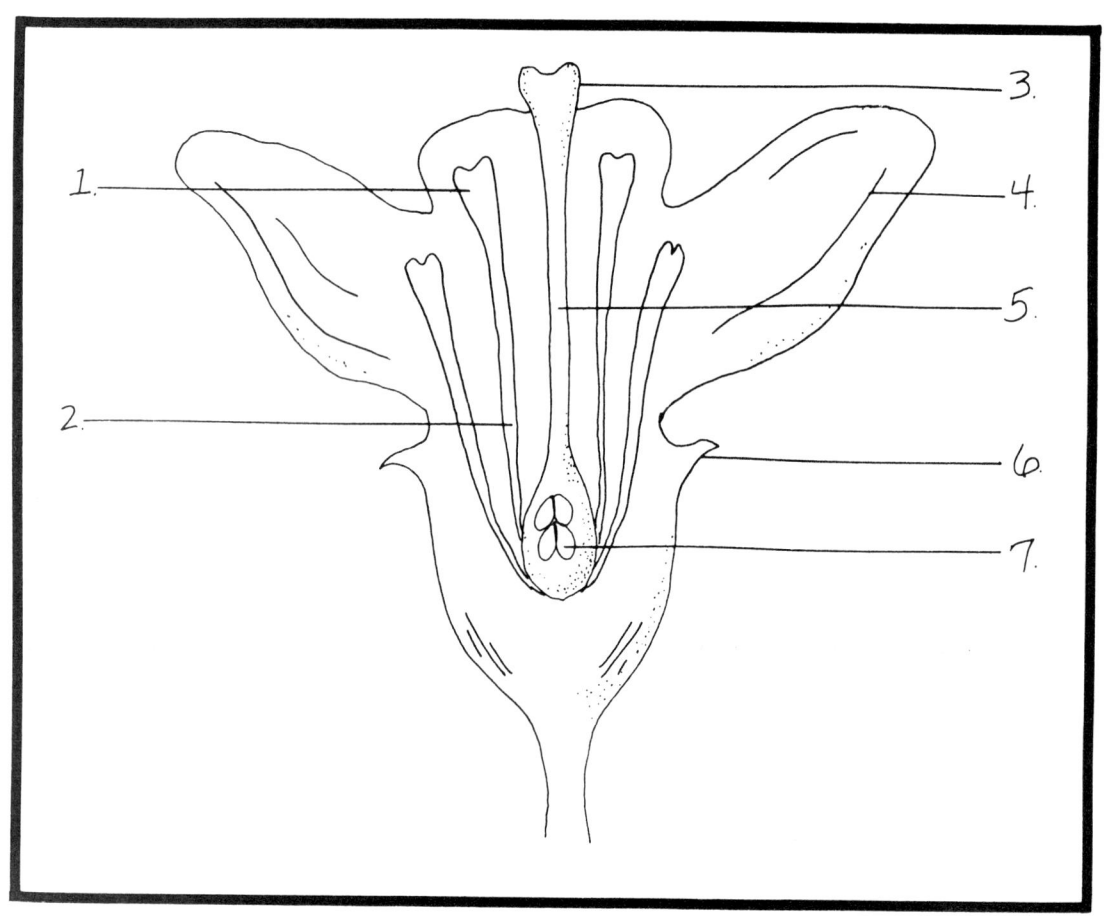

Label the parts of the flower above, then answer the following questions:

1. Which two parts of the above flower are male reproductive organs? _____ and _____

2. Which three parts of the above flower are female reproductive organs? _____ , _____ , and _____
    _____

3. Where are the seeds formed? _____

4. Where is the pollen formed? _____

5. Which two parts protect the reproductive organs of the flower? _____ and _____

6. If the above flower is fragrant and colorful, how may it be pollinated? Why? _____

7. Is the above flower likely to be self-pollinated? Why?
    _____

8. Now examine the flowers which were brought in for dissecting. Look for the above parts and decide how these flowers would most likely be pollinated.

9.   What is a staminate flower? _____

_____

10.   What is a pistillate flower? _____

_____

11.   Are any of your lab sample flowers staminate? _____

12.   Are any of your lab sample flowers pistillate? _____

13.   What are the names of your sample flowers? _____

_____

_____

14.   In the space below draw and label a sample flower from
      your lab.

WHAT IS GERMINATION

PURPOSE: Germination means to sprout, to begin devel-
opment and growth. The purpose of this activity is
to show students that each seed planted does not
necessarily develop and grow. This activity will also
enable students to understand the term percentage
of germination.

MATERIALS: This activity can be done in two ways:
students can actually test seed germination by planting
easy-to-grow seeds such as beans, or they may simply
use the provided diagram.

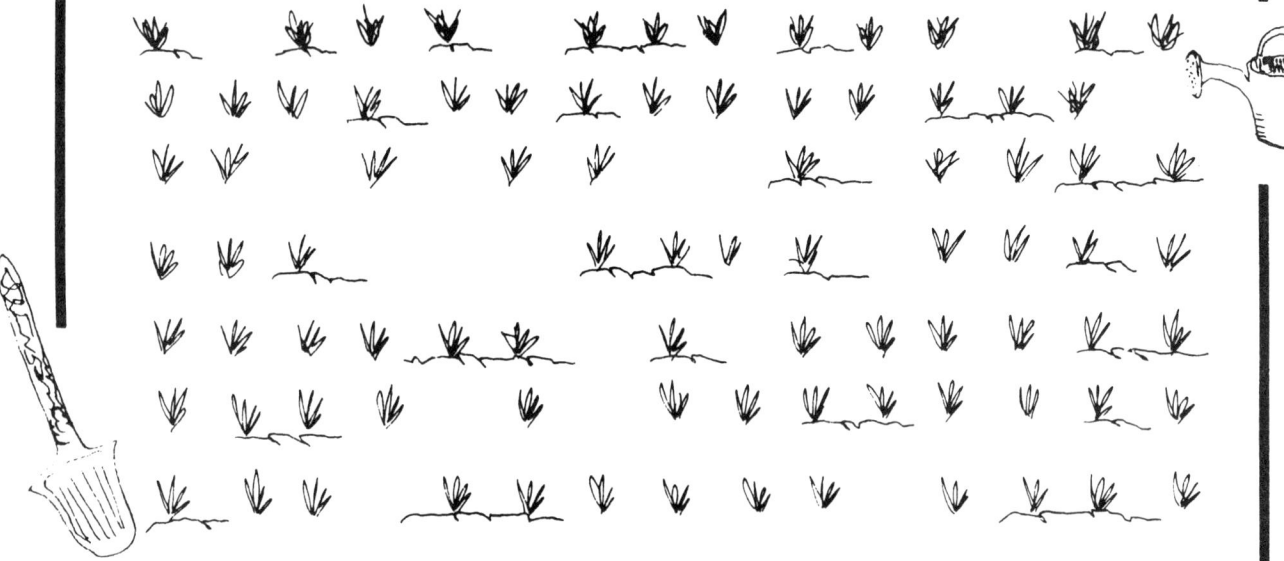

Mr. Smith planted 100 melon seeds; after a couple
of weeks the seeds began to grow. Out of curiosity
Mr. Smith counted the plants which grew. Using the
above drawing, answer the following questions:

9

1. How many melon seeds germinated? _____

2. How many did not germinate? _____

3. What was the percentage of germination? _____

4. What percentage did not germinate? _____

5. What conditions are necessary for germination? _____

_____

6. What are some things that Mr. Smith could do to help germination? _____

_____

7. Are there reasons beyond Mr. Smith's control for some seeds
   not germinating? _____

8. What might these reasons be? _____

_____

9. Explain, as you understand it, the term germination. _____

_____

10. Examine some seed packets. Look for information concerning
    germination, or data giving percentage of germination.
    If this information is available, plot it on the bar graph
    below.

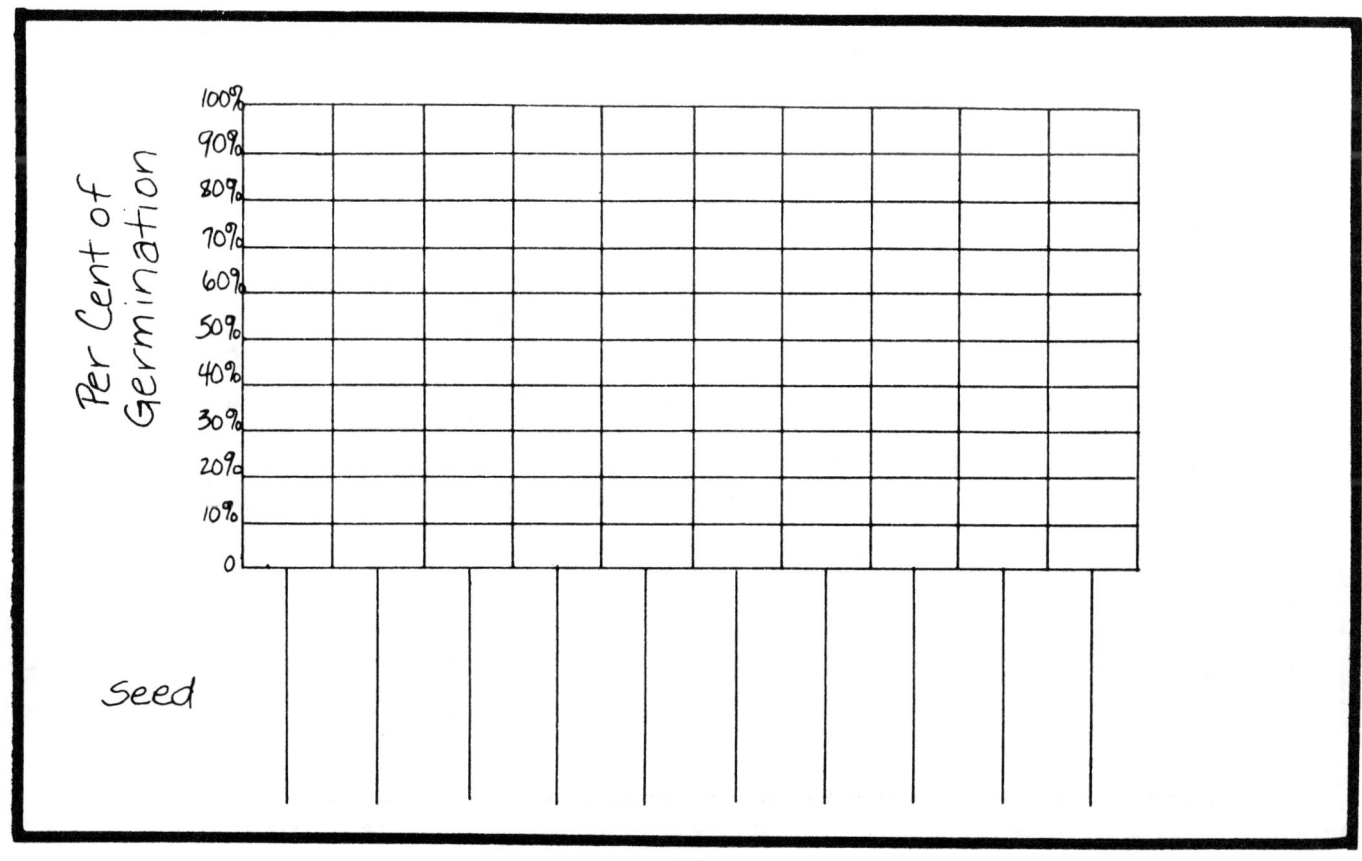

A MELON EXPLOSION!

PURPOSE: To illustrate by means of a hypothetical melon the fact that in nature living things reproduce in such quantities that if all were to survive, the results could mean a population explosion!

MATERIALS: Drawing as provided, or fresh fruits or vegetables which are easily dissected, such as corn, beans, or green peppers, paper towels, razors or knives.

PROCEDURE: Cut open the fruit or vegetable provided. Be careful to save all the seeds. If you are using the drawing, count the seeds in the drawing. Answer the following questions:

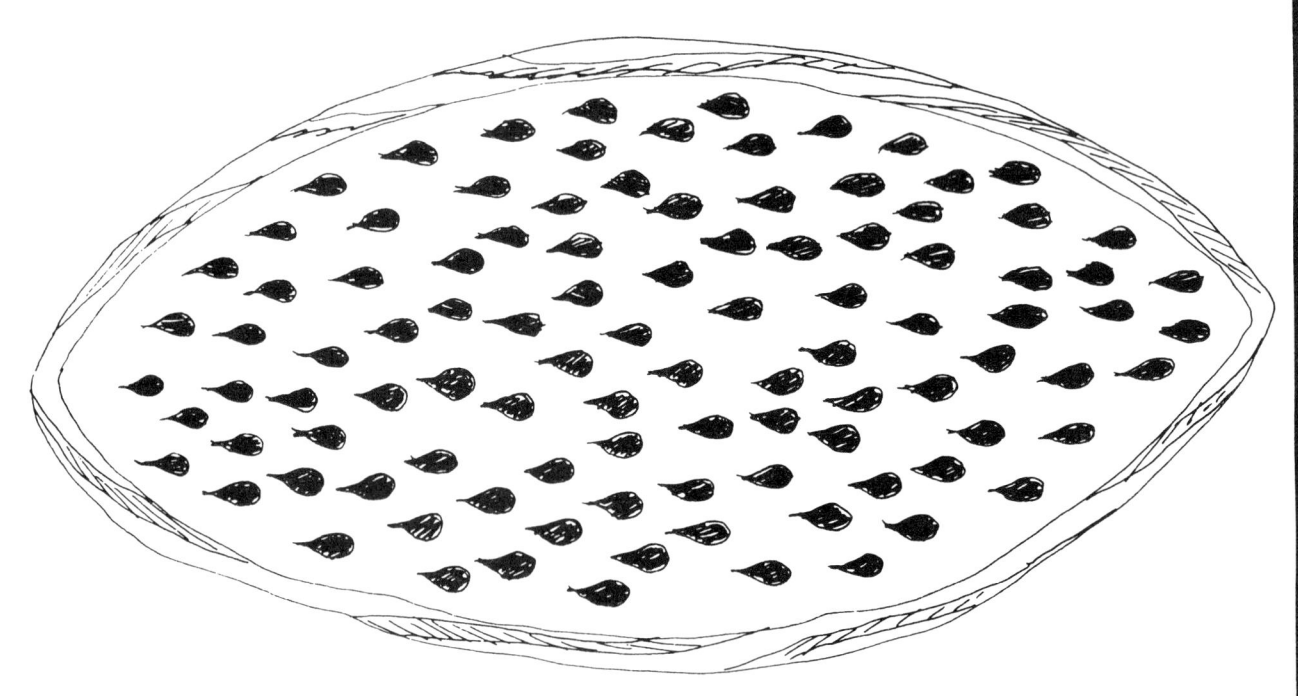

A MELON EXPLOSION! - WORKSHEET

1. The number of seeds in the melon is _____ .

2. If all the seeds in this melon germinated successfully, how many new plants would there be next year? _____

3. If each new melon plant produced ten melons on its vine and each melon produced 100 seeds and these seeds germinated, how many new plants would we have now? _____

4. All seeds do not germinate. Why is this fortunate? _____
   _____
   _____

5. Of the seeds that do germinate, many plants die before they bear fruit. What are some possible causes that might result in the death of these plants? _____
   _____
   _____

6. Some fish, such as the cod, are capable of laying over a million eggs. Compare the cod to the melon. _____
   _____
   _____

7. Why are the oceans not teeming with cod? _____
   _____
   _____

8. What is meant by the term "population explosion"? _____
   _____
   _____

TRANSPORTATION OF WATER IN CELERY

PURPOSE: To demonstrate vividly the transportation of water through the xylem cells of a plant stem.

MATERIALS: Celery stalks, beakers, red ink, blue ink, or both.

PROCEDURE: Trim a quarter of an inch off the bottom of celery stalks, and allow leaves to stay intact. Place stems in beakers with ink. Make observations several hours later and the next day. Allow to stand several days.

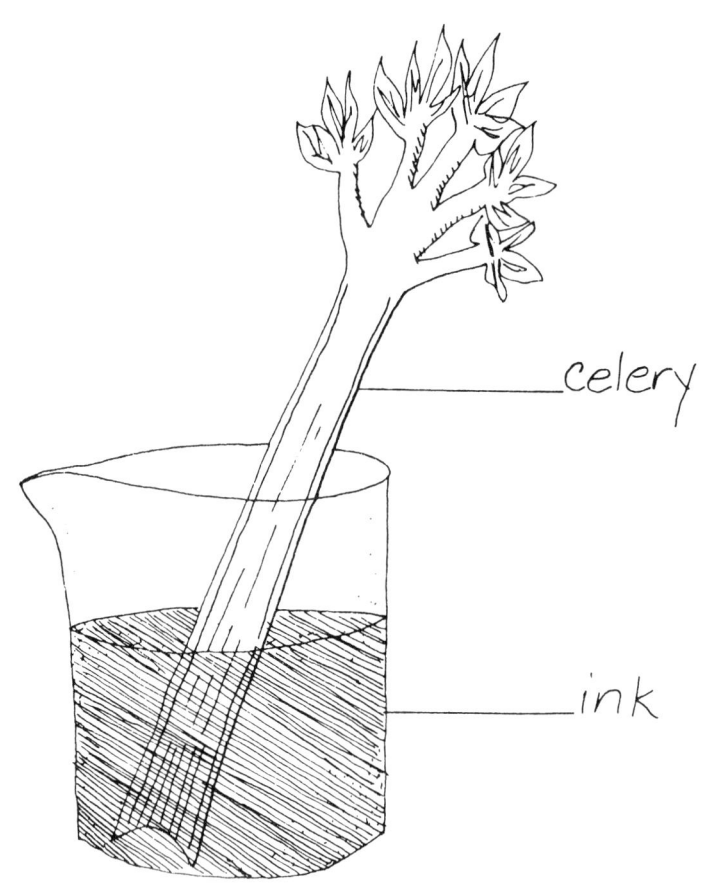

Observations: _____

_____

_____

_____

_____

_____

Transportation of Water in Plants

This experiment can be varied by changing the colors of inks or food colorings and by splitting the stems of a variety of flowers. White carnations, shasta daisies, and white roses work well. Try splitting the stems in halves, thirds or quarters and dipping each section into a different color for several hours or overnight.

PURPOSE: The students will learn by doing some of the complexities which arise in classification.

MATERIALS: (For each student, or each team of students, the following items can be used, or the teacher may wish to make substitutions as he or she sees fit.) A paper sack to hold the items, a wooden toothpick, a piece of gravel or a small rock, a nail, a penny, a large seed such as a watermelon or lima bean, a checker or poker chip, a shell, a pencil, a birthday cake candle, etc.

ITEMS:

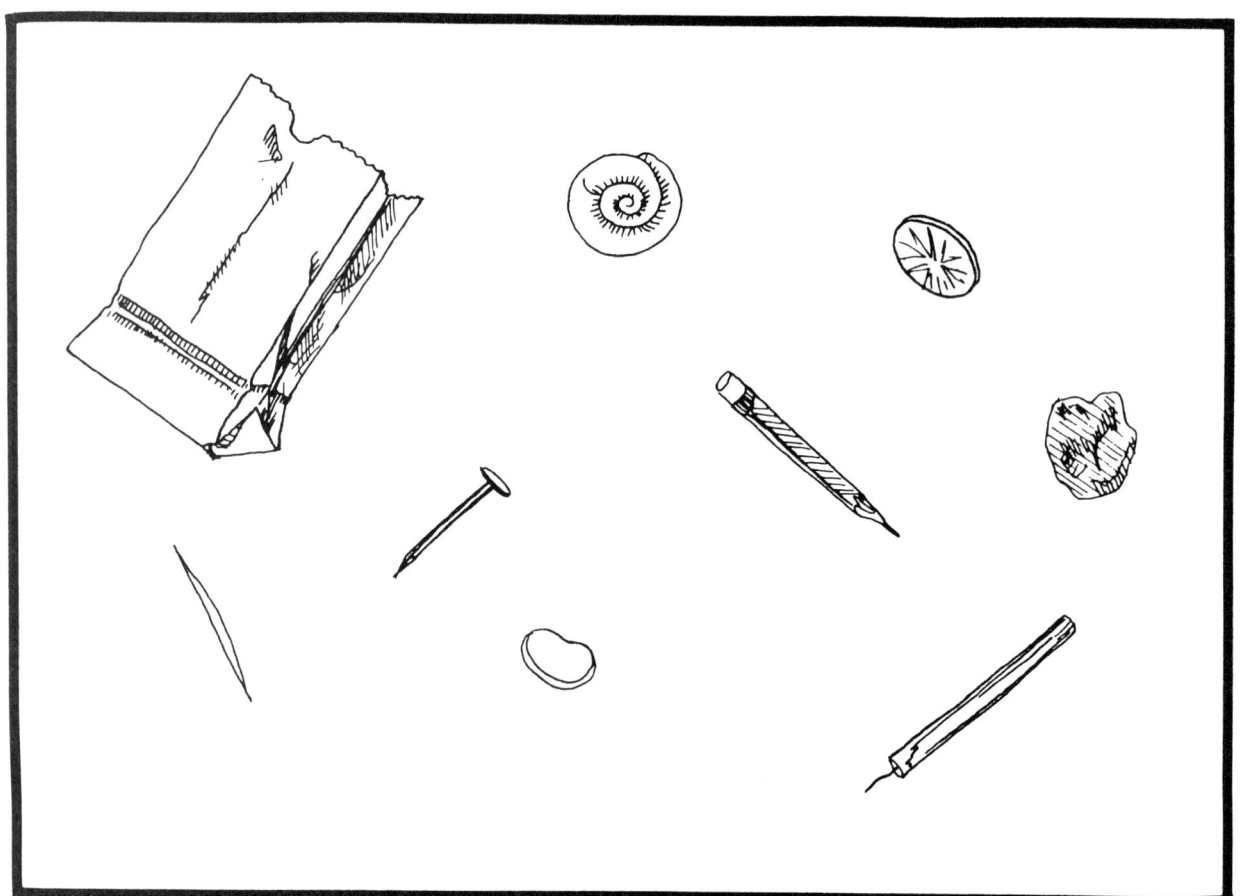

PROCEDURE: Ask the students to group or "classify" the objects in their sacks in any way they see fit. Allow students to have as many or as few groups as they wish. Give no hints or further instructions. The teacher may or may not want the students to write out their lists. When the students are finished, compare lists. The results will show that some students will classify according to color, some to size, some will group according to texture and combine the metals, the plastics, etc. Other students may put the objects into those which were once alive and those which never had life.

CONCLUSION: Tell the students there really are no correct answers to this exercise; the point of it was to demonstrate the fact that in the science of living things, classification can be difficult, that all scientists do not always agree, and that classification is a changing process as new information and evidence are acquired.

QUESTIONS FOR DISCUSSION:

1. Why did you classify the objects as you did?

2. Did other students classify the same way you did?

3. Did other students classify differently?

4. What are some of the problems scientists face in classifying living things such as plants?

5. Do you think scientists always agree when they classify living things?

6. Would a set of rules help guide both you and scientists when classifying?

HOW TO USE A SIMPLE KEY

PURPOSE: This is an activity using common everyday items put into a key in order to show students how scientists use keys. Trees, fish, insects, bacteria, and most living things can be identified by means of keys.

MATERIALS: Toothpick, nail, rock, penny, pencil, large seed, plastic checker or poker chip, shell, birthday cake candle. NOTE: These are the same items used in the activity entitled PROBLEMS OF CLASSIFI-CATION.

PROCEDURE: A key is a valuable tool for anyone interested in identifying living things. In using the key below the objects will have fictitious names. In order to use a key a student takes the information he knows about an object and follows the given descriptions. To find the new names for the objects, always start at 1A for each object. See if the description fits 1A or 1B, then move down the key as directed.

OBJECTS:

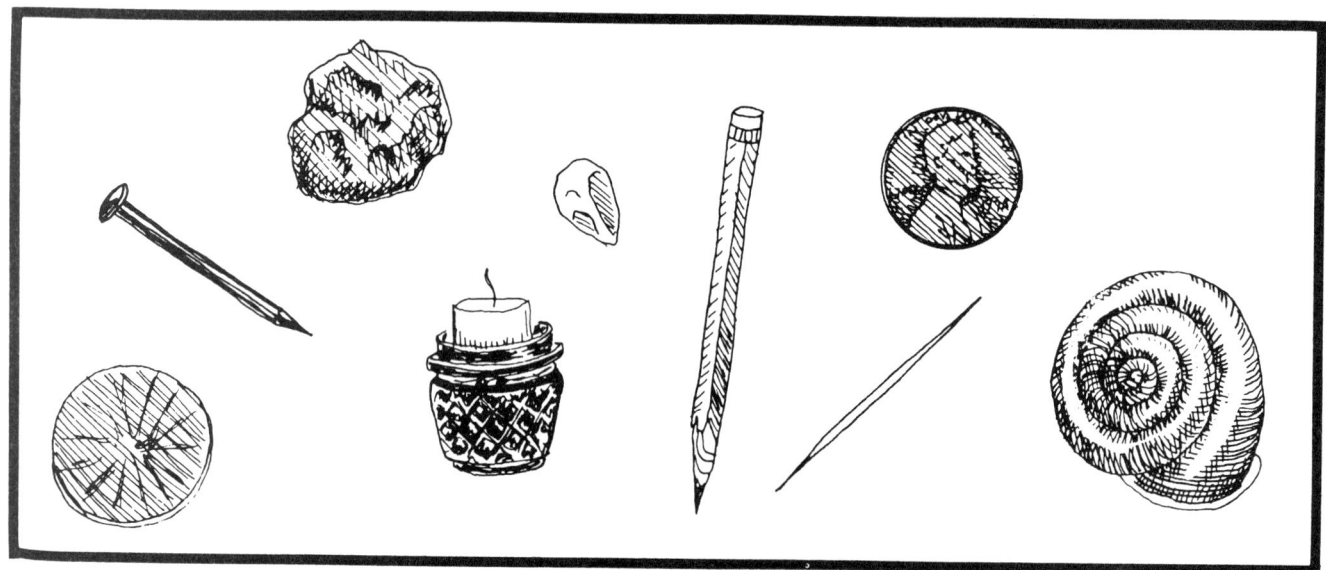

Key on the following page.

A SIMPLE KEY

1A Made of wax .... a nac
1B Not made of wax .... see 2

2A Slender and pointed .... see 3
2B Not slender and pointed .... see 4

3A Made of wood .... see 5
3B Not made of wood .... a lan

4A Round in shape .... see 6
4B Not round in shape .... see 7

5A Writes with a black mark .... a nep
5B Does not write .... a cip

6A Made of copper .... a ney
6B Made of plastic .... a rek

7A Was once living or part of a living thing .... see 8
7B Was not living or part of a living thing .... a cor

8A Part of a plant .... a des
8B Part of an animal .... a lel

After the students key out each object they decode the fictitious names into the real names. If the key was used properly the names will be decoded as follows:

     nac .... candle

     lan .... nail

     nep .... pencil

     cip .... toothpick

     ney .... penny

     rek .... checker

     cor .... rock

     des .... seed

     lel .... shell

NOTE: It is more effective to use the objects; however, pictures or drawings may take the place of the nine objects.

A TREE KEY

PURPOSE: To give students practice in using a key; to familiarize students with the characteristics of trees.

MATERIALS: Pictures or drawings as provided on the next page.

PROCEDURE: A key is a valuable tool to anyone interested in the identification of living things. In using a key a student takes all the information he is given about an object and follows the given steps. In order to find the name of the tree, always start at 1A for each tree, determine if the description 1A or 1B fits, then follow the key as directed.

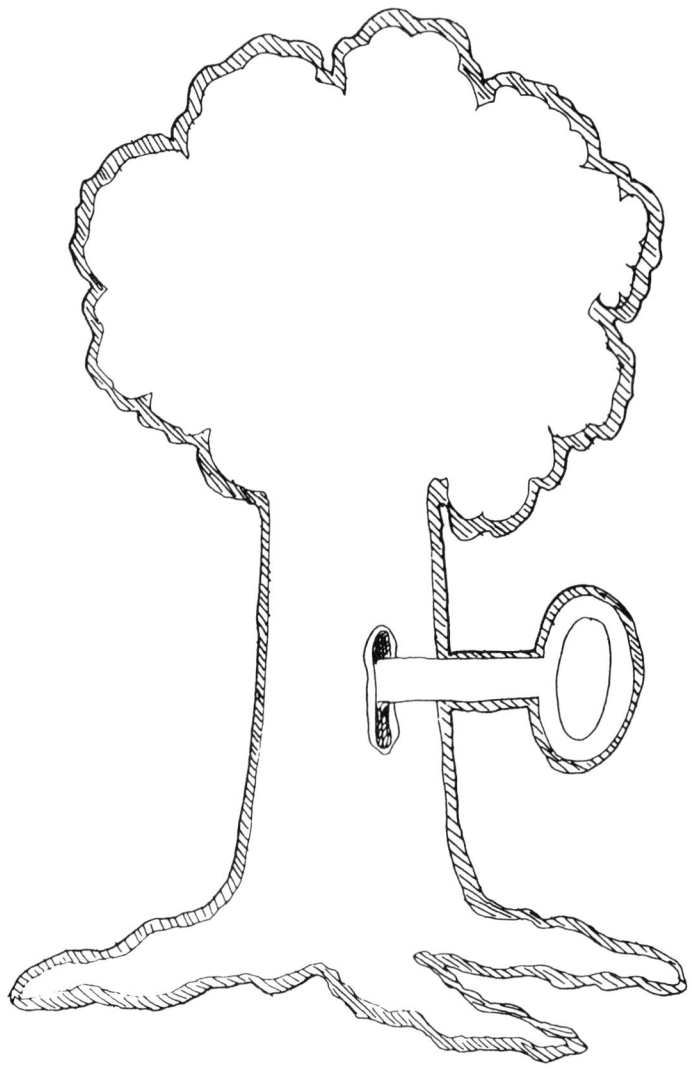

A SIMPLE TREE KEY

1A Trees with needle-like or scaly leaves .... See 5

1B Trees with flat leaves .... See 2

2A Trees with simple leaves not divided into leaflets ..... See 3

2B Trees with compound leaves divided into leaflets .... See 4

3A Edges of leaves smooth, no teeth or lobes .... Dogwood

3B Edges of leaves toothed .... American Elm

4A Leaflets arranged like a feather .... Black Walnut

4B Leaflets arranged in a circle .... Horse Chestnut

5A Needles long, three to a cluster .... Longleaf Pine

5B Needles short, compact, arranged in spirals
       around stem .... Black Spruce

TREE	NAME
a.	
b.	
c.	
d.	
e.	
f.	

BIOTIC FIELD TRIP

PURPOSE: To observe and record the interrelationships of organisms in a particular community.

MATERIALS: Record sheet, pencil or pen.

PROCEDURE: Record the evidence on the data sheet as observed.

BIOTIC FOOD CHAIN

FIELD TRIP

1. List the food producers you see on your field trip.

   _____
   _____
   _____

2. List the plant and animal consumers you find on your field trip.

   _____
   _____
   _____

3. Describe the biotic factors of the field trip community.

   _____
   _____
   _____

4. Draw or describe a food chain you observed in the field trip community.

   _____
   _____
   _____

5. Fill in the steps of a food pyramid you observed.

6. Look for and describe examples of (a) mutualism, (b) commensalism, (c) parasitism, (d) competition.

   _____
   _____
   _____
   _____

23

Use this page to fill in a food pyramid and food chain which you observed on your field trip.

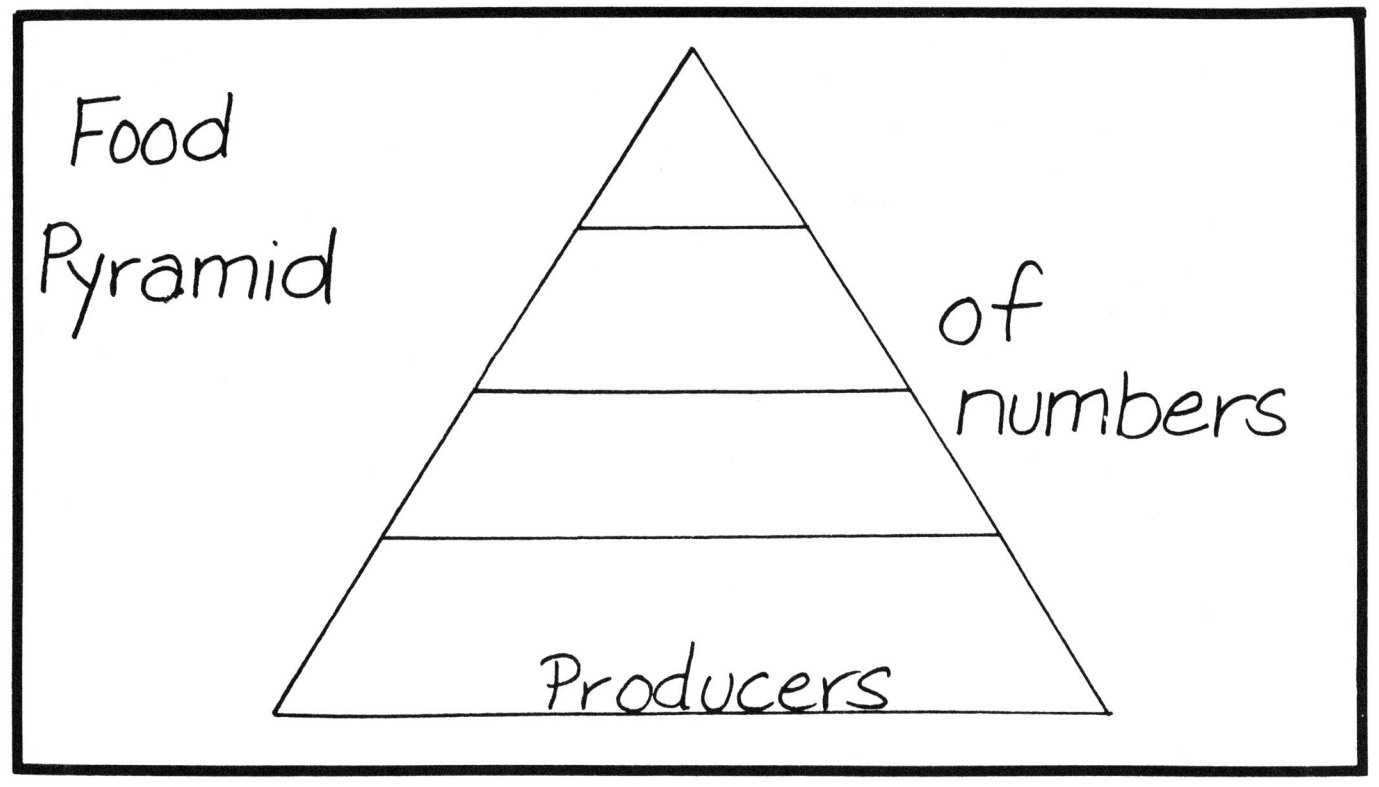

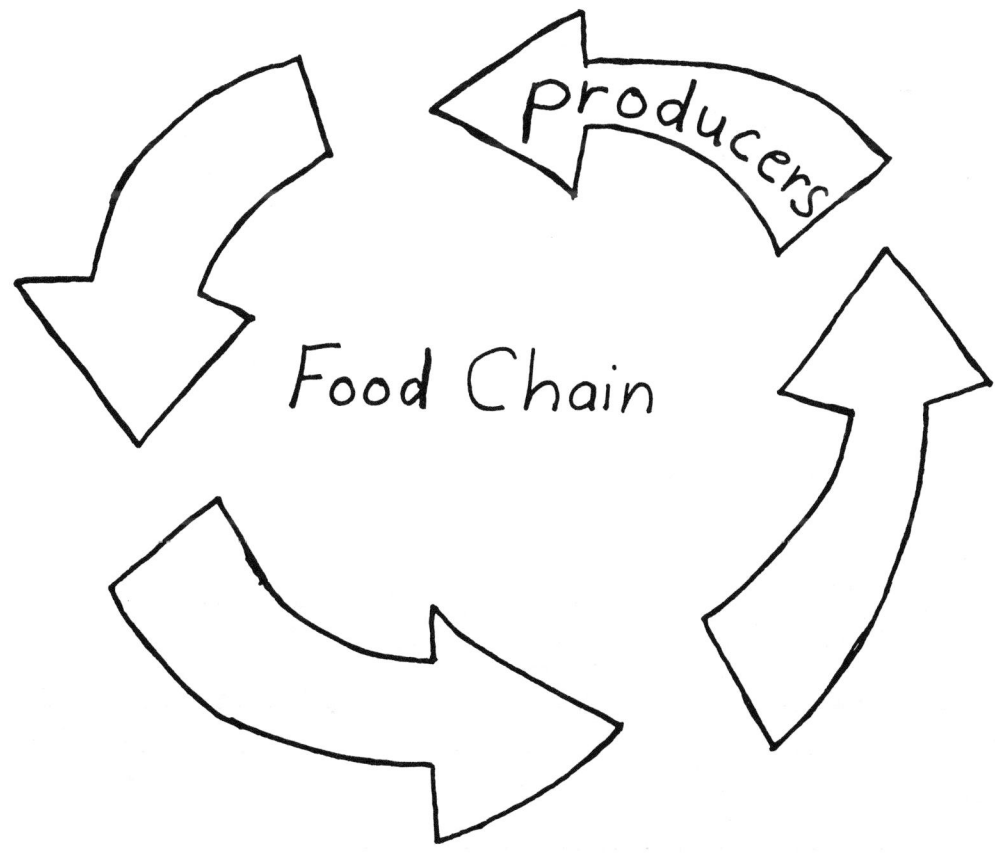

MAKING A LEAF COLLECTION

PURPOSE: During a field trip or as a special project on plants students will benefit from the study and identification of a leaf collection.

MATERIALS: Leaves, wax paper, old magazines, iron.

PROCEDURE: As you collect fresh leaves place them between the pages of a magazine. Later press the leaves between sheets of paper with a warm iron. Identify and mount on construction paper.

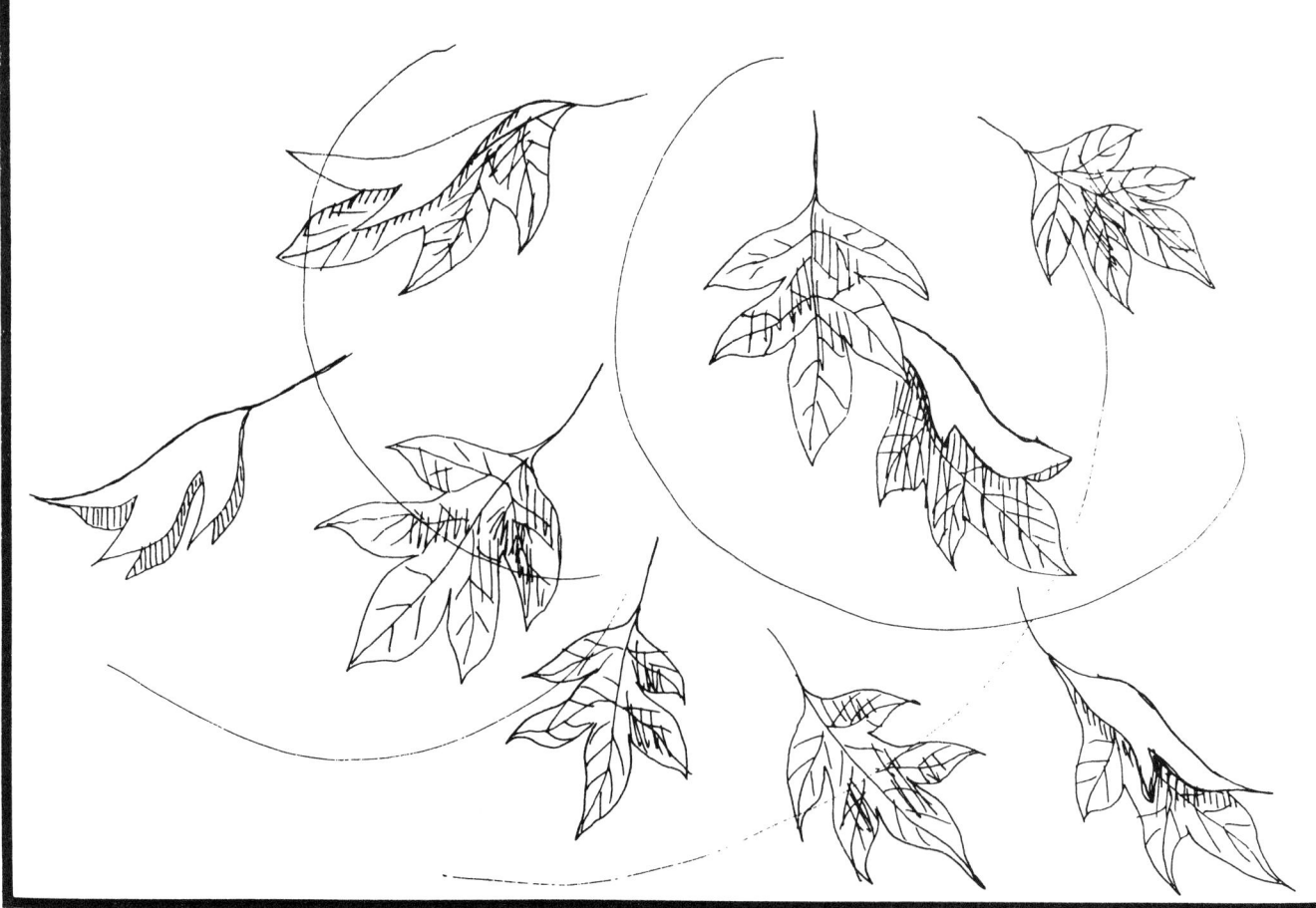

TREE SILHOUETTES

PURPOSE: To determine whether students can match tree forms to the correct name of the tree. This exercise can be used as a classroom exercise, follow-up exercise after a field trip, or as a quiz.

MATERIALS: Tree silhouettes; reference texts may be needed.

PROCEDURE: Many people are able to identify a tree by its leaf or bark, but can you identify a tree by its form or silhouette? Some basic tree forms are: vase , broad or spreading , columnar , oval , and weeping . Match each form on the next page to the tree's name.

Silhouette   Name

1. _____   _____

2. _____   _____

3. _____   _____

4. _____   _____

5. _____   _____

Find other examples of each of the tree forms.

Vase _____

Spreading _____

Columnar _____

Oval _____

Weeping _____

Match the tree silhouette to the tree tags below.

Columnar

Spreading

Vase

Weeping

Oval

Weeping Willow

American Elm

Lombardy Poplar

White Oak

Sugar Maple

PLANT DRAWINGS

PURPOSE: To provide guide sheets for some of the most commonly studied plant structures.

MATERIALS: Guide sheets, pen or pencil.

PROCEDURE: Sheets can be used for the study of plants in the lab or in conjunction with microscope activities.

Monocot Germination
Guide Sheet

Dicot Germination
Guide Sheet

Guide Sheet

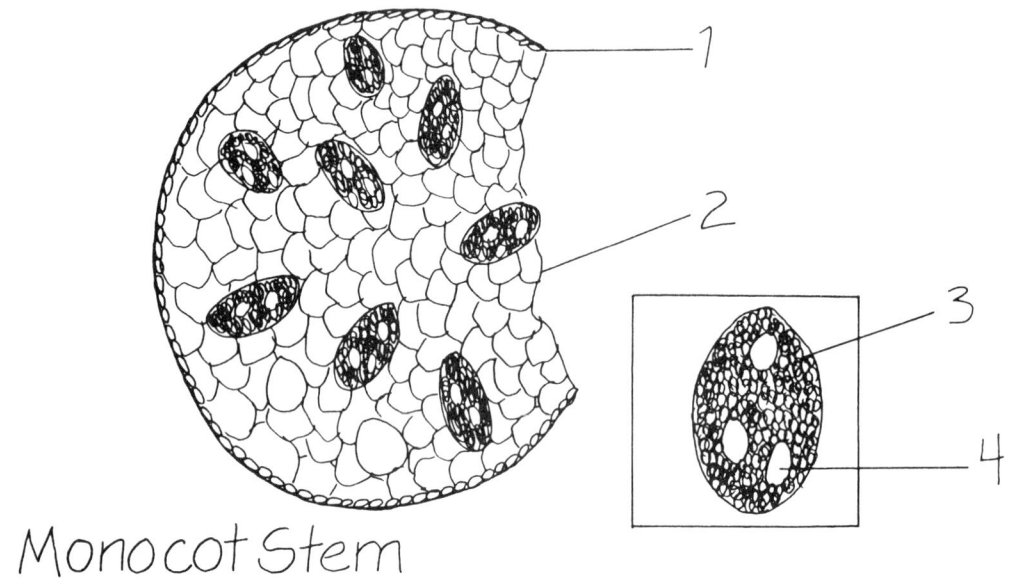

Monocot Stem

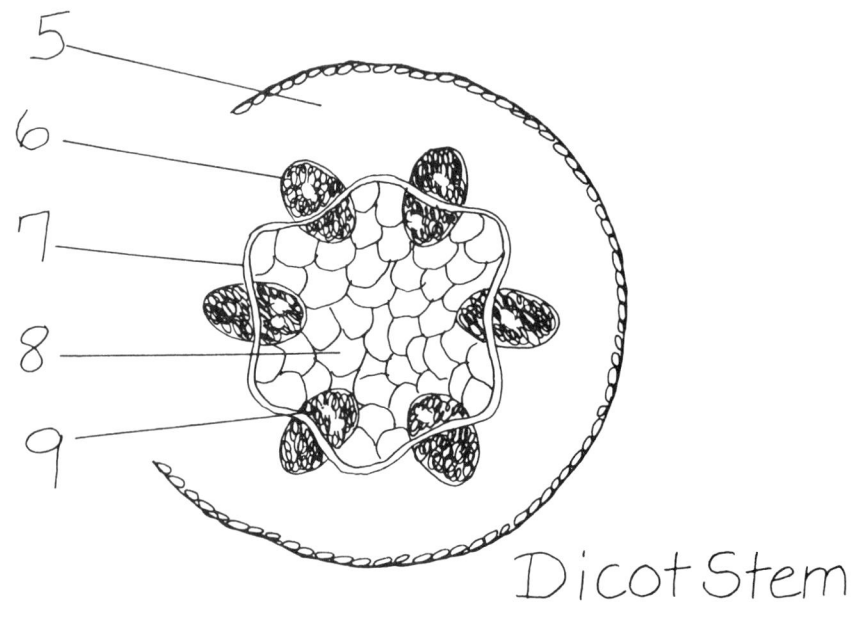

Dicot Stem

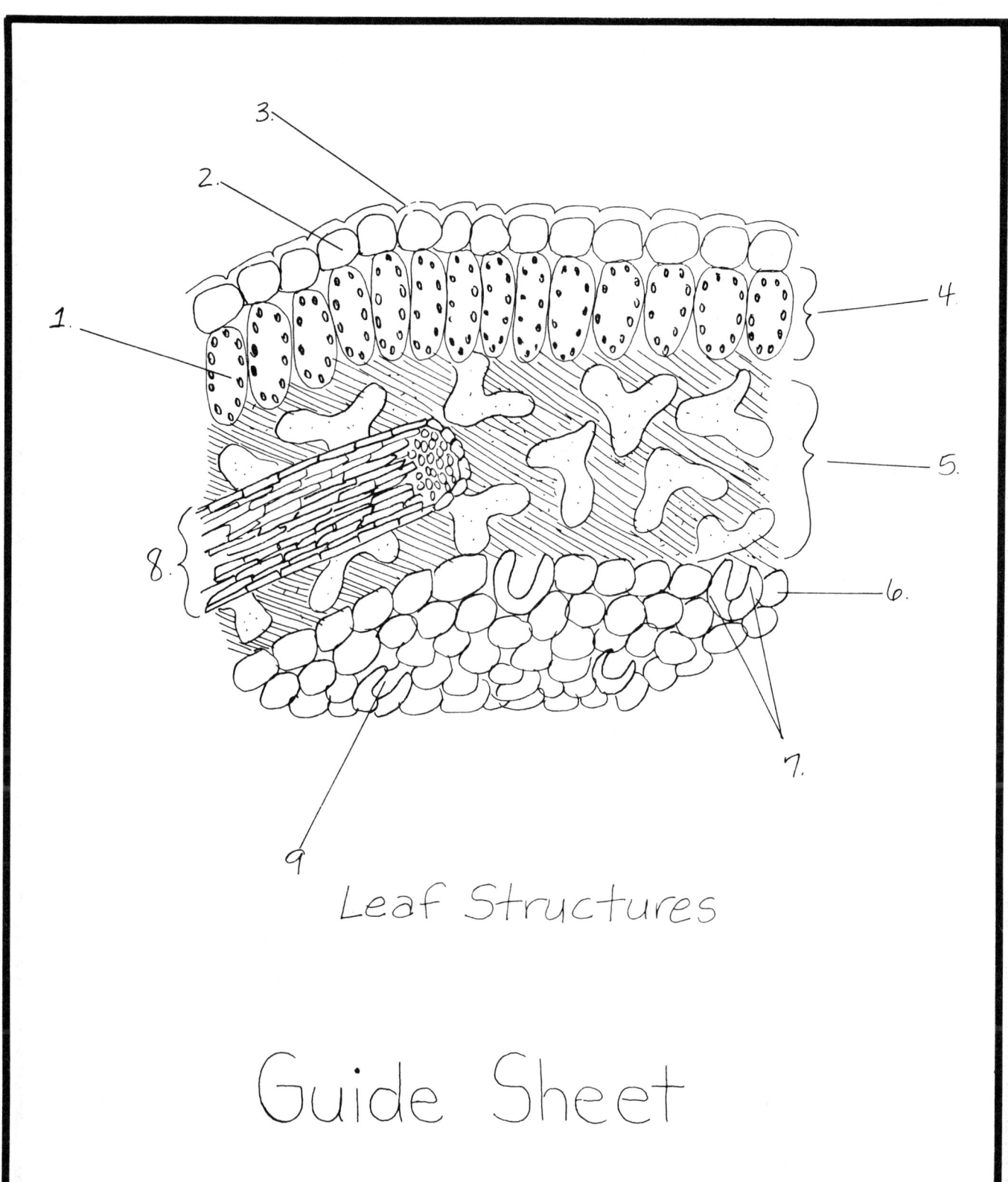

Leaf Structures

Guide Sheet

Guide Sheet

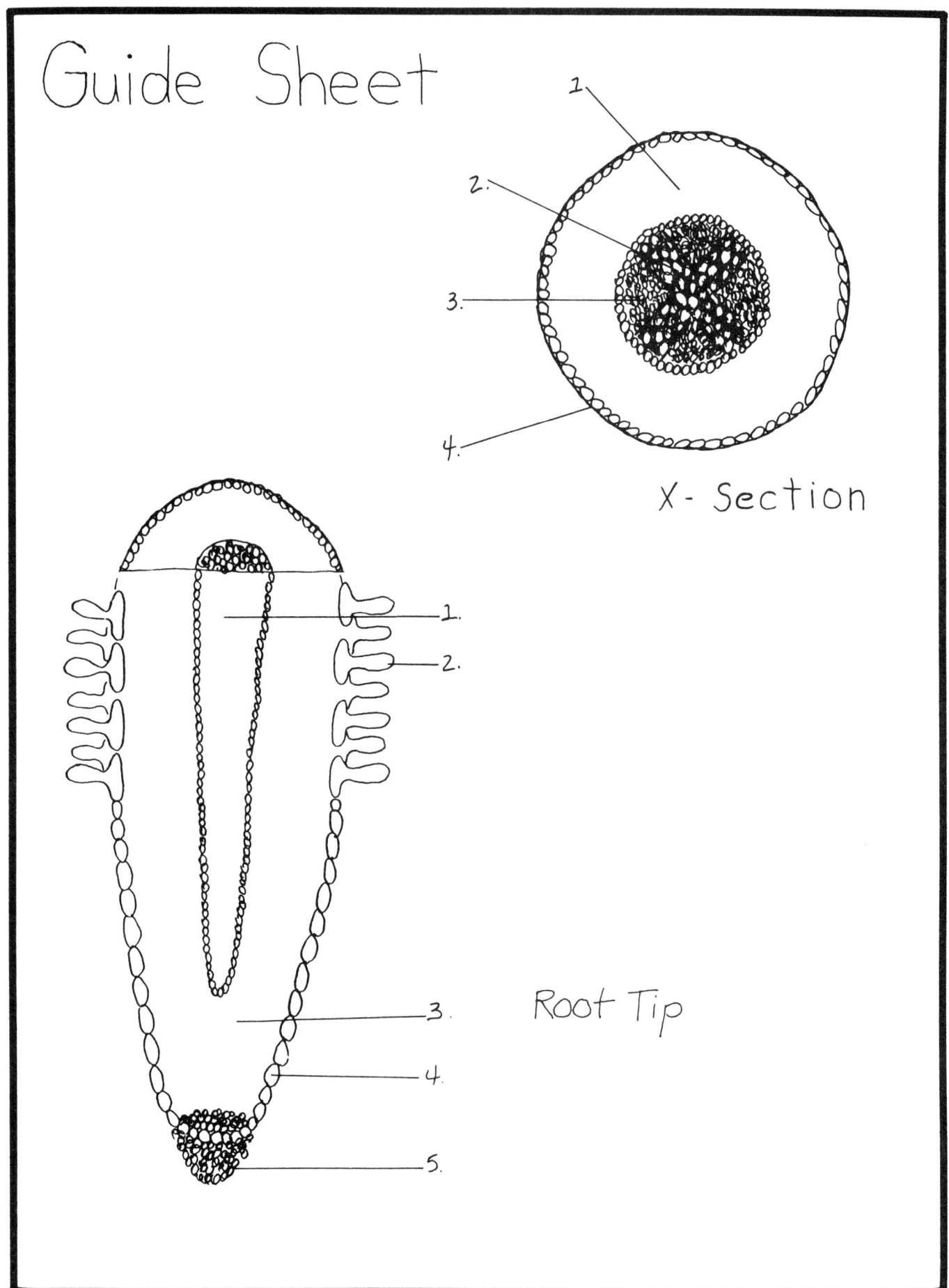

X- Section

Root Tip

ROTATION SEED LAB

PURPOSE: This lab is designed to make students think of the different types of seeds, their coverings, their size, identification, means of transportation, uses, etc.

MATERIALS: A variety of seeds, glue, 3" x 5" cards. Some of the easily available seeds which can be used are: lemon, orange, apple, pumpkin, grass, pecan, walnut, sycamore, peas, beans, corn, hickory, poppy, hemlock, pine, pepper, tomatoes, Brazil nut, chestnuts, poplar, dandelion, oak (acorn), okra, mace, cardamon, marigold, rose, plum, peach, almond, watermelon, etc. Attach seeds to cards with glue and label. Each seed is a station.

PROCEDURE: Students rotate in lab stations and fill out information sheet on the next page. Students change stations when time to change is indicated by the teacher.

SUGGESTION: Variety is the key to this lab. Select seeds which differ in size, mode of being transported, and those with a variety of coverings. Nuts are especially interesting if they have the soft covering which is over the shell as in the case of the black walnut. Dandelion and maple seeds are interesting because they are wind-borne; the dandelion seed is shaped similar to a parachute, and the maple seed is similar to wings. Rulers can also be useful. If available, provide them for students at each station so that the seeds can be measured metrically.

Name of seed	Mode of transportation				Coverings			
	wind	insects	large animals or man	water	fleshy	shell or nut	thin	naked
1.								
2.								
3.								
4.								
5.								
6.								
7.								
8.								
9.								
10.								
11.								
12.								
13.								
14.								
15.								
16.								
17.								
18.								
19.								
20.								
21.								
22.								
23.								
24.								
25.								
26.								
27.								
28.								
29.								
30.								

TREE DATING-NATURE'S CALENDAR

PURPOSE: To show how we can determine the age of old lumber by using a board of known age, grown in the same locality as the lumber of unknown age.

MATERIALS: Drawings of lumber which show the annual rings. These drawings can be put on ditto paper as in the example or on strips of white cardboard. (The strips of cardboard are very easy to work with.) A section of the annual rings must coincide with both lumber samples. Scissors.

PROCEDURE: Cut the paper down the center with Beam A and Beam B on separate strips. Match up the annual rings. The place where the annual rings coincide tell us that these trees were growing at the same time and experienced the same rainfall, temperatures, droughts, etc. If the age of one beam or board is known, this information can be used to tell something about the unknown board. Now answer the following questions:

1.   In what year was tree A planted? _____

2.   In what year was tree A harvested? _____

3.   How many years did tree A and tree B grow concurrently? _____

4.   In what year was tree B planted? _____

5.   How many years old was tree A when it was harvested? _____

6.   How many years old was tree B when it was harvested? _____

7.   Which two years were the best growing years for tree A? _____

8.   Which were the best years for tree B? _____

_____

Guide Sheet

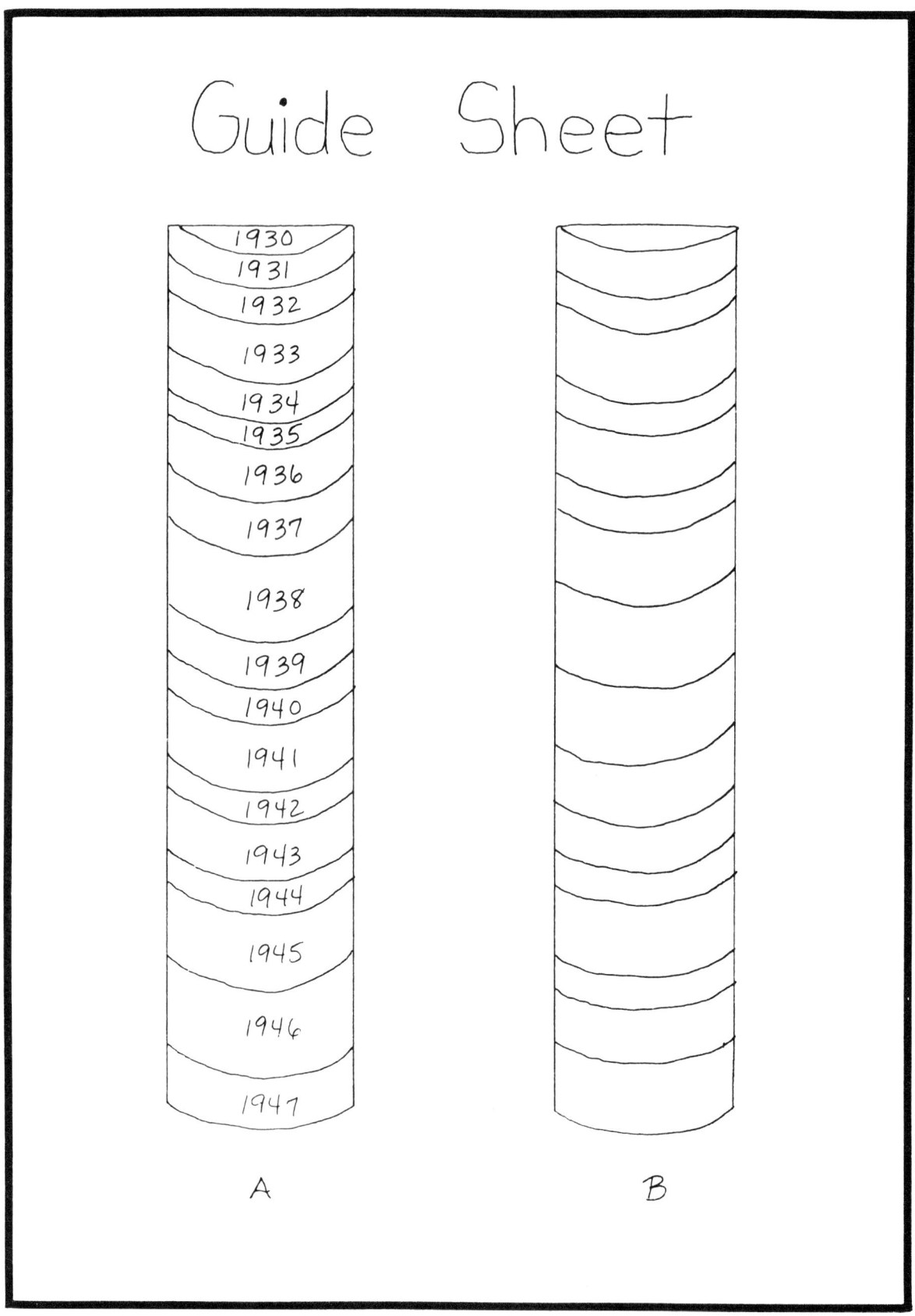

1930
1931
1932
1933
1934
1935
1936
1937
1938
1939
1940
1941
1942
1943
1944
1945
1946
1947

A

B

TREE CALENDARS

PURPOSE: Performing this exercise imparts much information to the students concerning how trees grow, which years were favorable for growth, etc. It also helps in the identification of trees.

MATERIALS: Cross sections of various trees, straight pins, flags made of stiff paper.

PROCEDURE: Obtain cross-sections of tree trunks. Have students make the tree calendars by looking up information in science, social studies, etc. Print the dates and occasions on the flags and pin in appropriate places on the tree cross-sections.

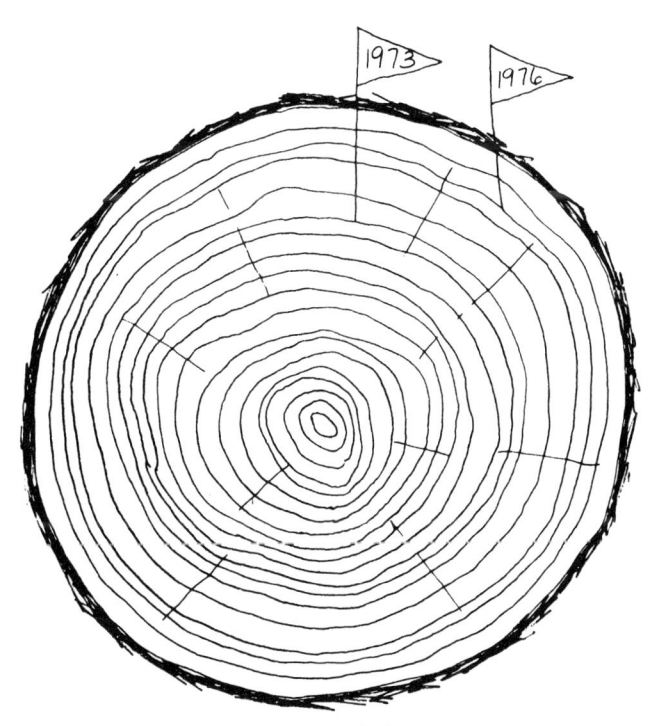

REPEAT A FAMOUS EXPERIMENT OF ROBERT HOOKE

PURPOSE: To repeat a very simple experiment which was a milestone in science. To learn something of the life of Robert Hooke.

MATERIALS: Microscope, razor, cork, glass slide.

PROCEDURE: Make an exceedingly thin slice of cork and examine it microscopically. Draw what you see. Can you understand why Hooke called the individual parts of tissue "cells"? Check an encyclopedia entry for Robert Hooke and tell or write something about him.

CORK CELLS

COLOR THEM POISONOUS

PURPOSE: To make students aware that a variety of common plants are toxic to the extent that ingestion of their various parts can be FATAL.

MATERIALS: The given information, colored pen, pencils, or magic markers.

PROCEDURE: Below are some common plants, all of which have been known to cause death. Read the given information; color as directed.

This is a poinsettia; its flowers are so pretty at Christmas time; its leaves are fatal. Color the flowers red, pink, or white; leaves are green.

This is an oleander; its narrow green leaves and branches affect the heart and digestive system. It can cause death. Color the flowers white, pink, purple, or red.

All parts of a jimson weed are toxic, including its funnel-shaped flowers, which range in color from white to bluish-purple.

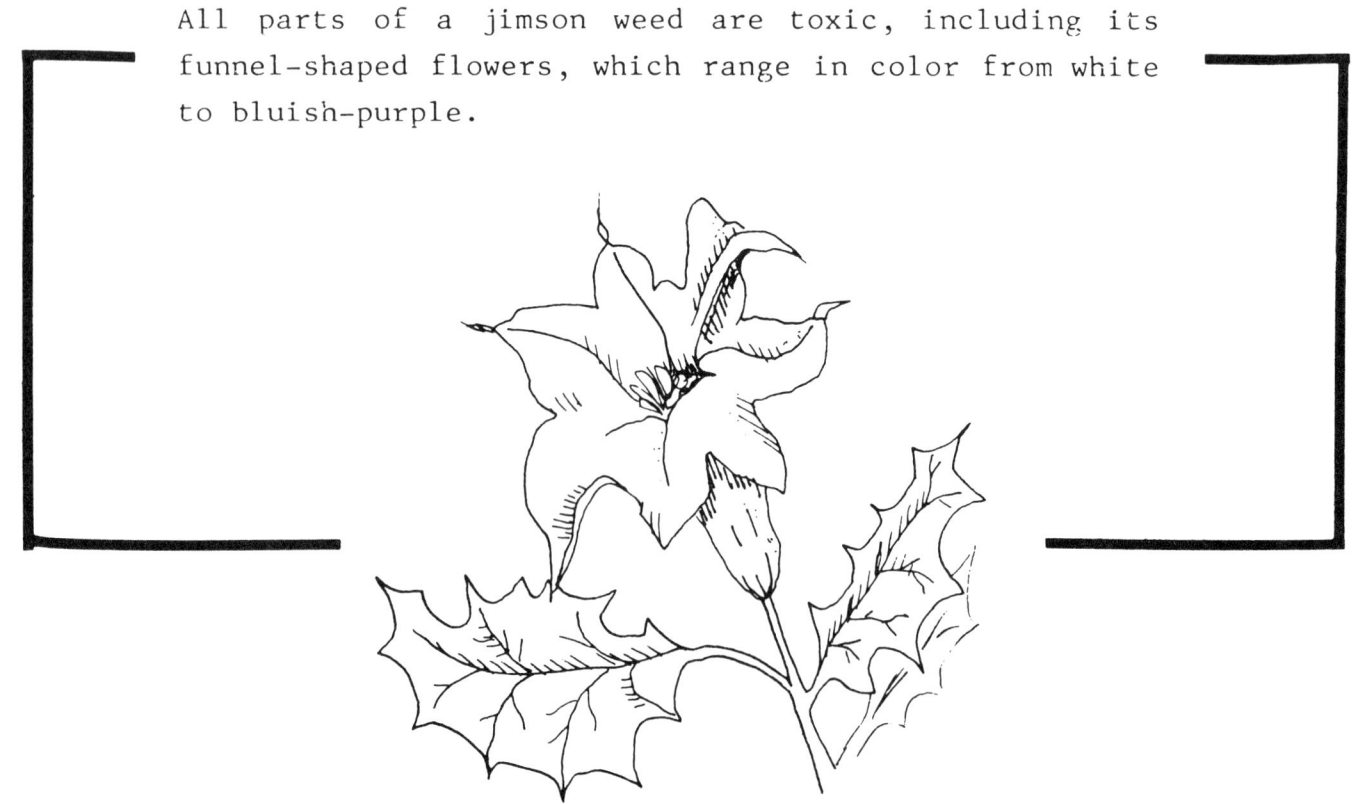

Azalea is a popular shrub, all parts of which can
be fatal. Leaves, flowers, and stems cause nausea,
vomiting, depression, coma, and possible death. Colors
of the flowers vary from white to many shades of pink,
red, or purple.

Yew is an evergreen shrub; its wood is highly prized
for archer's bows, but its berries and foliage can
be fatal. Berries are red; foliage is green.

This is rhubarb; its stems are edible; its leaves can cause convulsions, coma, even death. Color the stems pinkish-red; leaves are green.

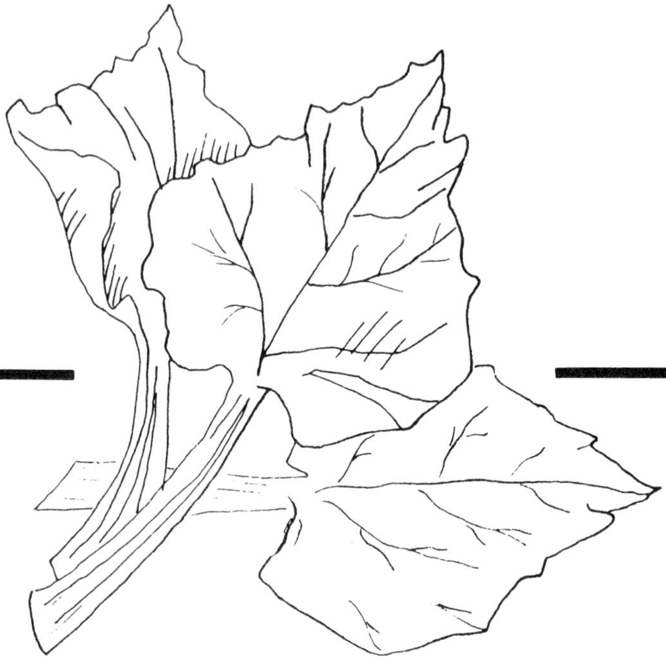

Standing under the mistletoe may earn you a kiss at Christmas time; however, be cautious of this plant. The berries are toxic; color them white; leaves are green.

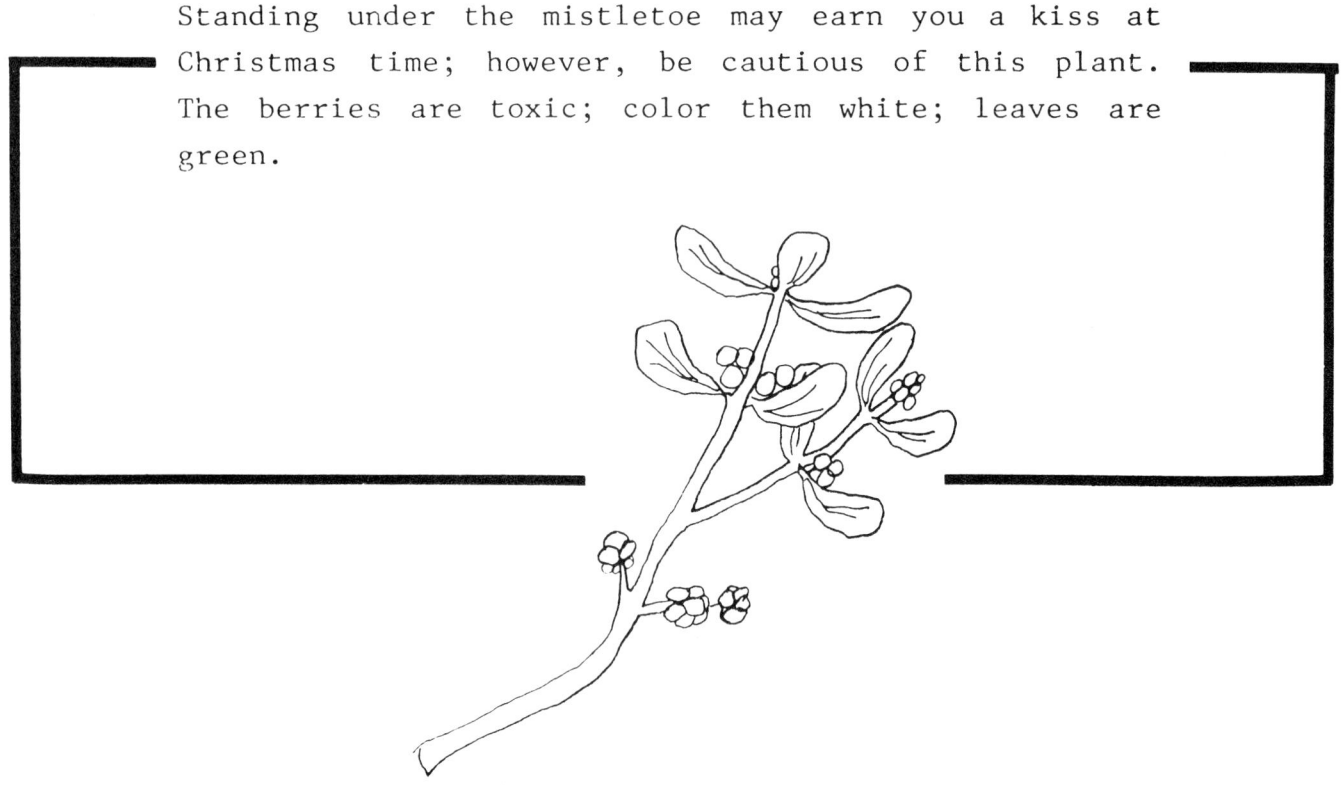

BUILDING A SUGAR MOLECULE

PURPOSE: To illustrate by counting the atoms, how green plants take six CO_2 molecules and six H_2O molecules and by the process of photosynthesis manufacture glucose $(C_6H_{12}O_6)$ and (CO_2).

MATERIALS: Quarter-size circles of construction paper in black, red, and white. For each student 18 red circles are needed to represent oxygen, 12 white circles to represent hydrogen, and 6 black circles to represent carbon. If you wish, toothpicks can be used to represent bonds.

PROCEDURE: Students will first build six CO_2 molecules and six H_2O molecules, as illustrated below. Do this on the first map sheet.

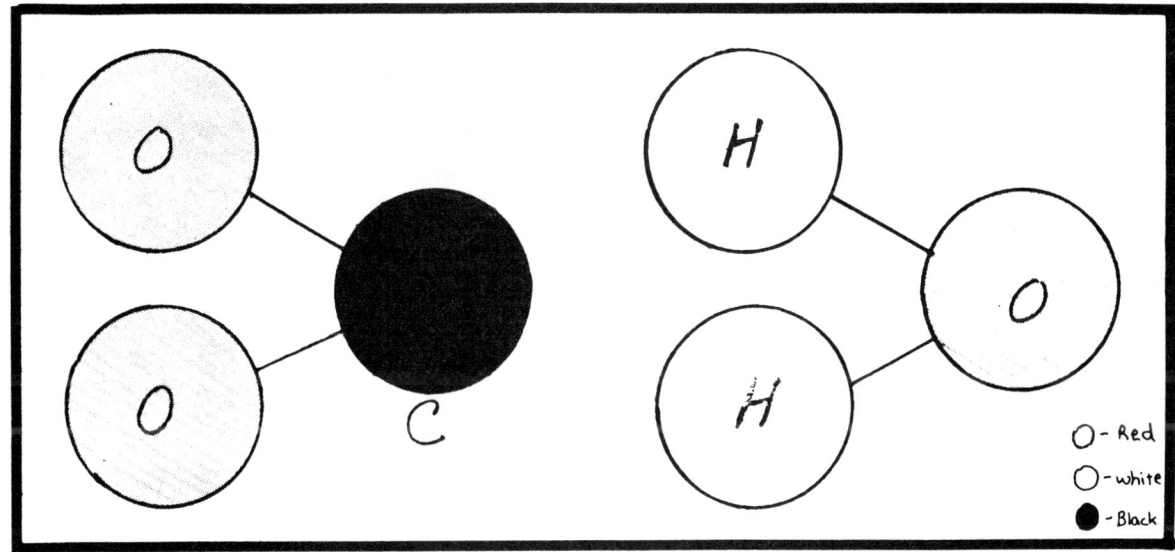

All extra circles must be put aside.

Students may not use any other circles except the ones which were used to build the six carbon dioxide molecules and the six water molecules.

Now the twelve molecules are taken apart.

With only the circles from the twelve molecules and using the map provided, students will build a sugar molecule and answer the following questions:

44

BUILDING A SUGAR MOLECULE - WORKSHEET

1. How many molecules are left over? _____

2. What color are they ? _____

3. What does this color represent? _____

4. When does this happen in nature? _____

5. Write a formula for this reaction. _____

6. Write a conclusion. _____

_____

_____

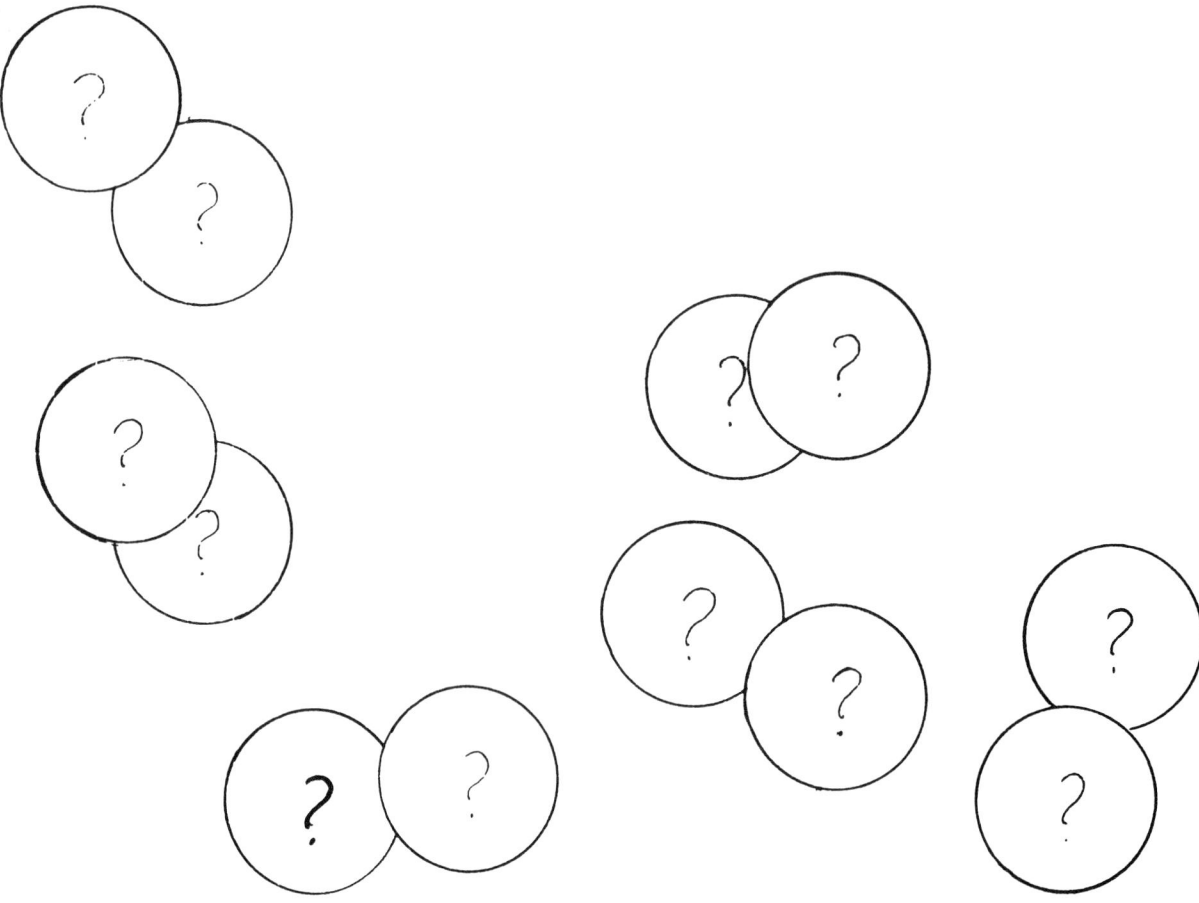

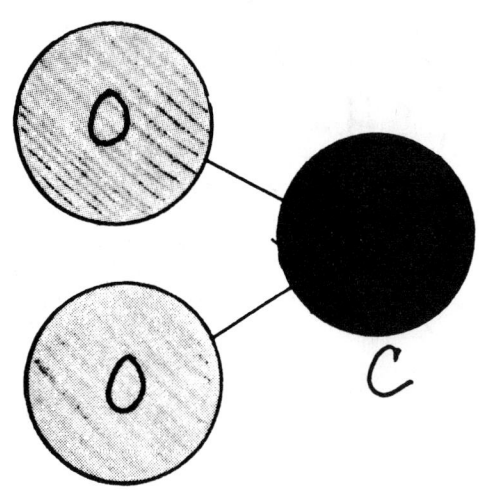
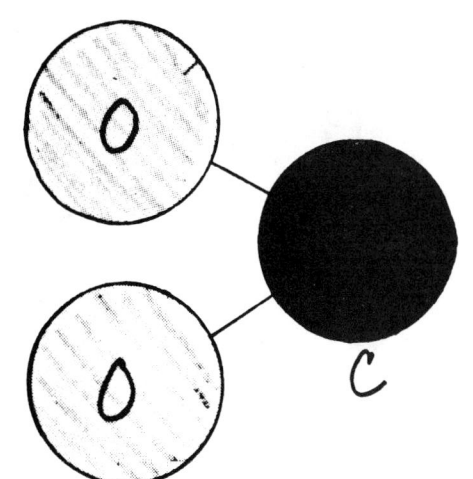

6 CO₂ (Carbon dioxide) molecules

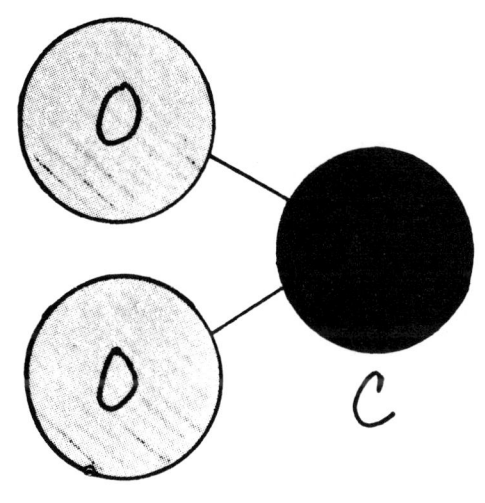
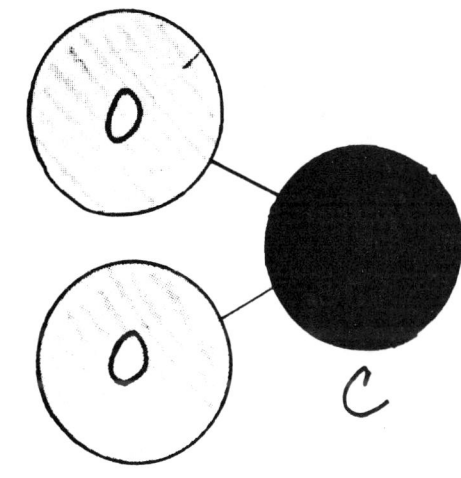

O - Red
O - White
● - Black

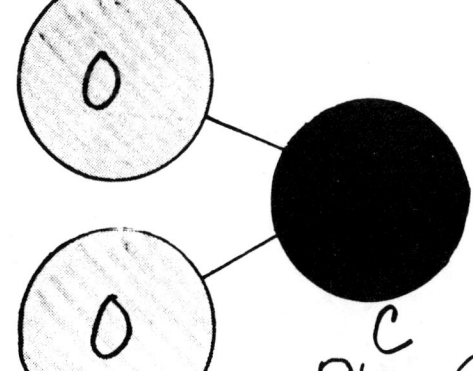
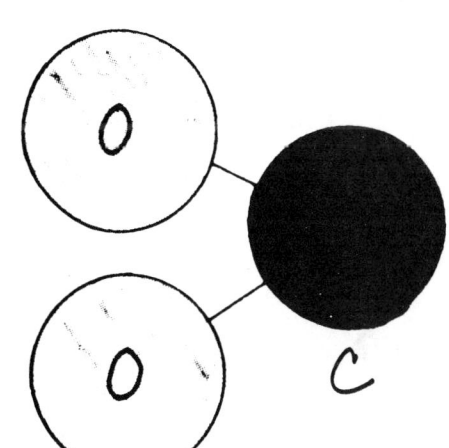

Plus (next page)

46

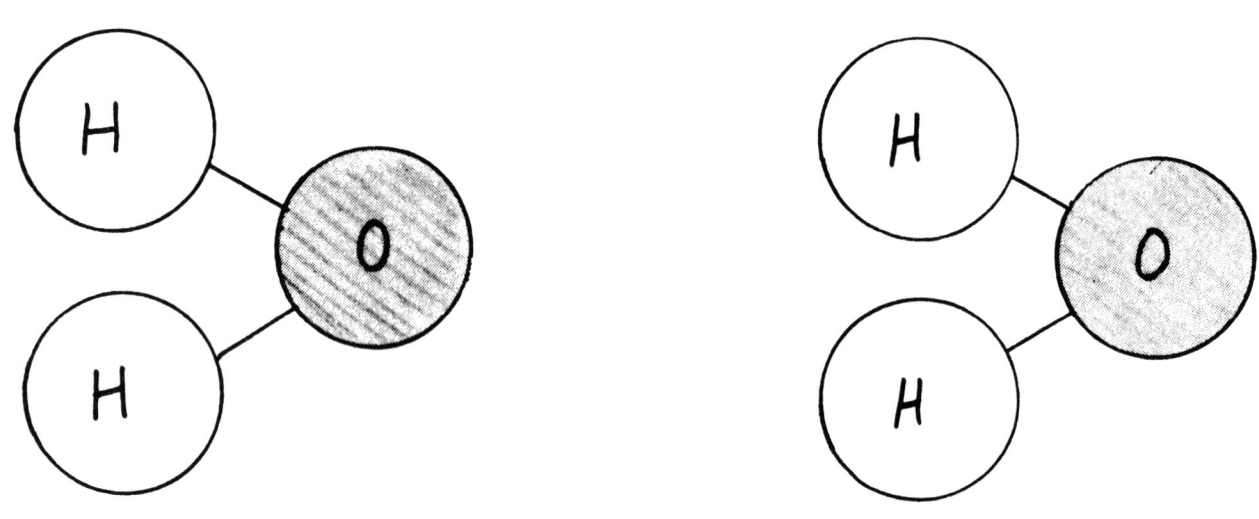

6 H$_2$O (water) molecules

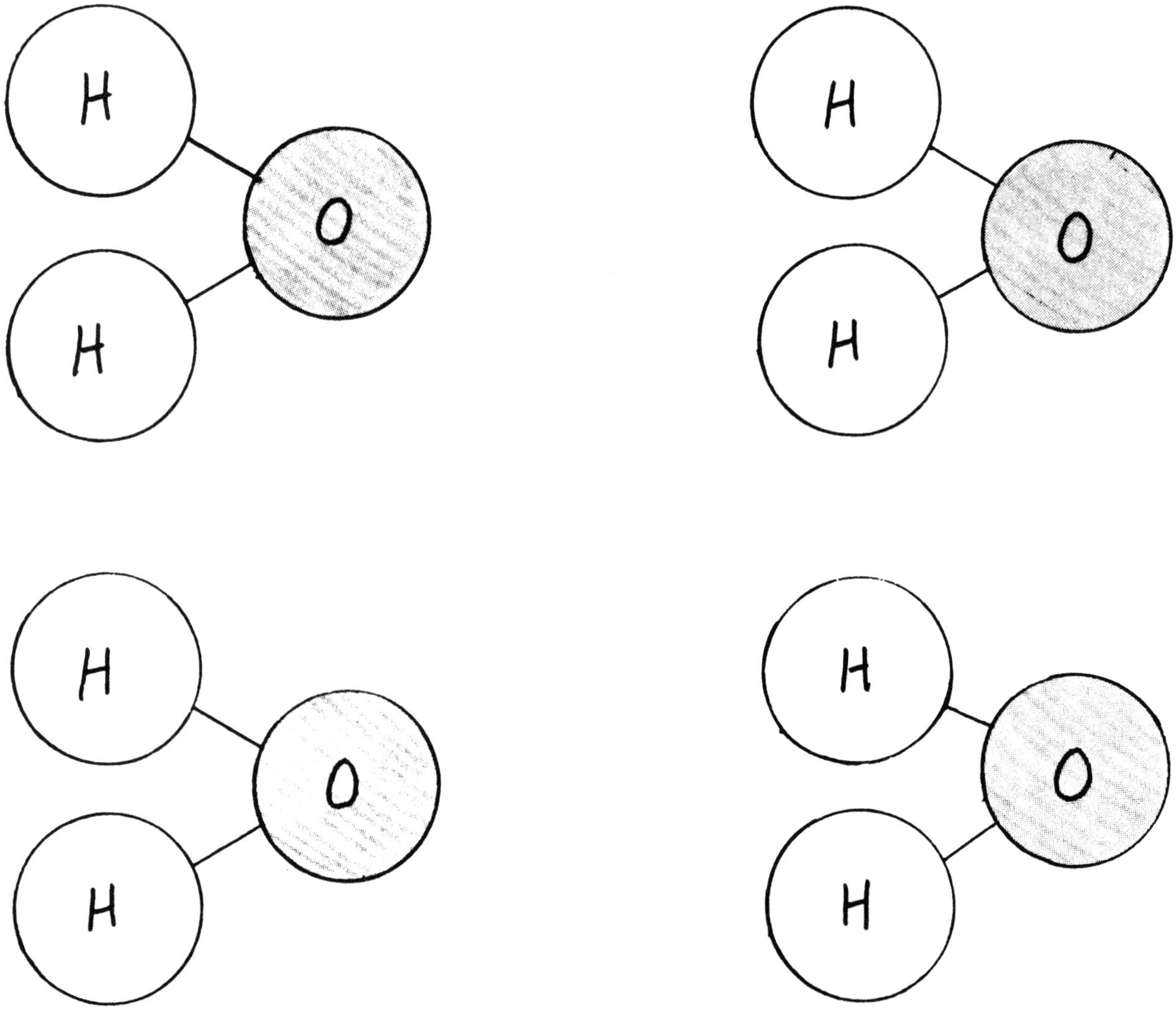

equal (next page)

Sugar (Glucose) Molecule Map

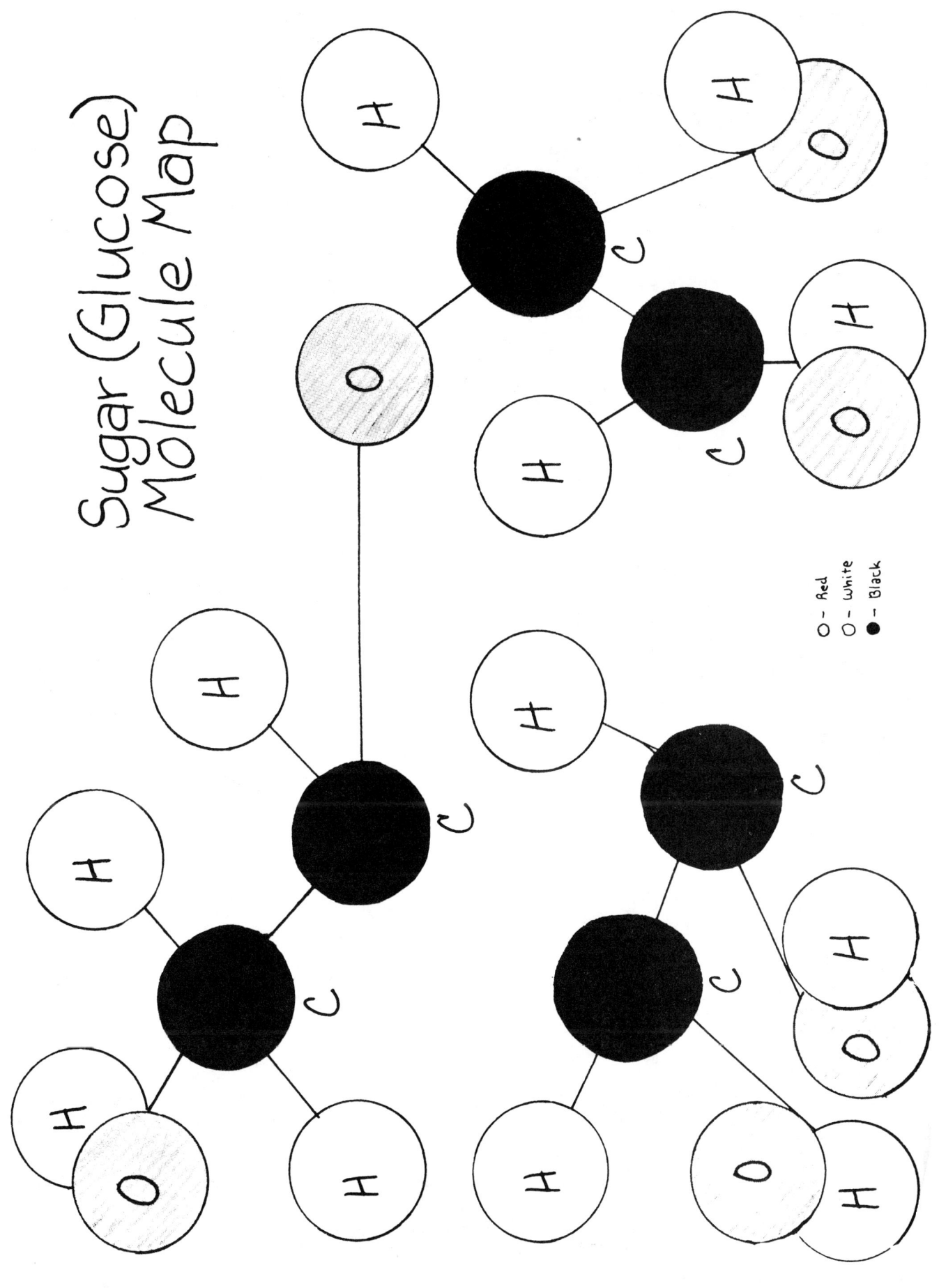

O – Red
O – White
● – Black

TREE BINGO

From the list below choose your favorite trees to make a unique bingo card. When your teacher calls out the tree names on your card, cross them out to get TREE BINGO!

Pecan, Ash, Yellow wood, Locust, Sumac, Sassafras, Mulberry, Ginkgo, Holly, Poplar, Sweewtbay, Box-elder, Coffee, Catalpa, Paulownia, Walnut, Buckeye, Oak, Bur oak, Lombardy poplar, Aspen, Pine, Birch, Tupelo, Gum, Nannyberry, Dogwood, Sourwood, Persimmon, Hackberry, Cherry, Chestnut, Peach, Apple, Willow, Maple, Hickory, Fir.

A NATURE FIELD TRIP

PURPOSE: This is a short descriptive outline for
the students to take on a field trip in order to make
the occasion more meaningful. It is also useful in
a post-field trip class discussion.

MATERIALS: Copy of outline, graph paper, and a pencil
or pen.

PROCEDURE: The outline is filled in by the students
as they make their observations. Other questions or
activities may be added. The graph paper is used to
indicate the lay of the land, streams or other bodies
of water, vegetation such as trees, shrubs, grass,
etc., and rocks and other inanimate objects.

NATURE FIELD TRIP

Name _____

1. Describe your field trip environment. _____
_____
_____

2. List five cultivated and five non-cultivated plants
which you see.

Cultivated	Non-cultivated
1. _____	1. _____
2. _____	2. _____
3. _____	3. _____
4. _____	4. _____
5. _____	5. _____

cont.

3. List five green plants and two non-green plants.

       Green Plants   Non-green Plants

    1. _____   1. _____

    2. _____   2. _____

    3. _____

    4. _____

    5. _____

4. List one or two aquatic plants, if present.

    1. _____

    2. _____

5. Take a handful of soil. Is it (a) sandy; (b) clay; (c) loam? (circle one)

6. List any animal life you see.

_____ _____

_____ _____ _____

_____ _____ _____

_____ _____ _____

7. Describe some physical factors you noticed on this trip.

_____

_____

_____

8. Make a map on the graph paper provided indicating the plants, large rocks, houses or barns, streams, places where you spotted animals, etc.

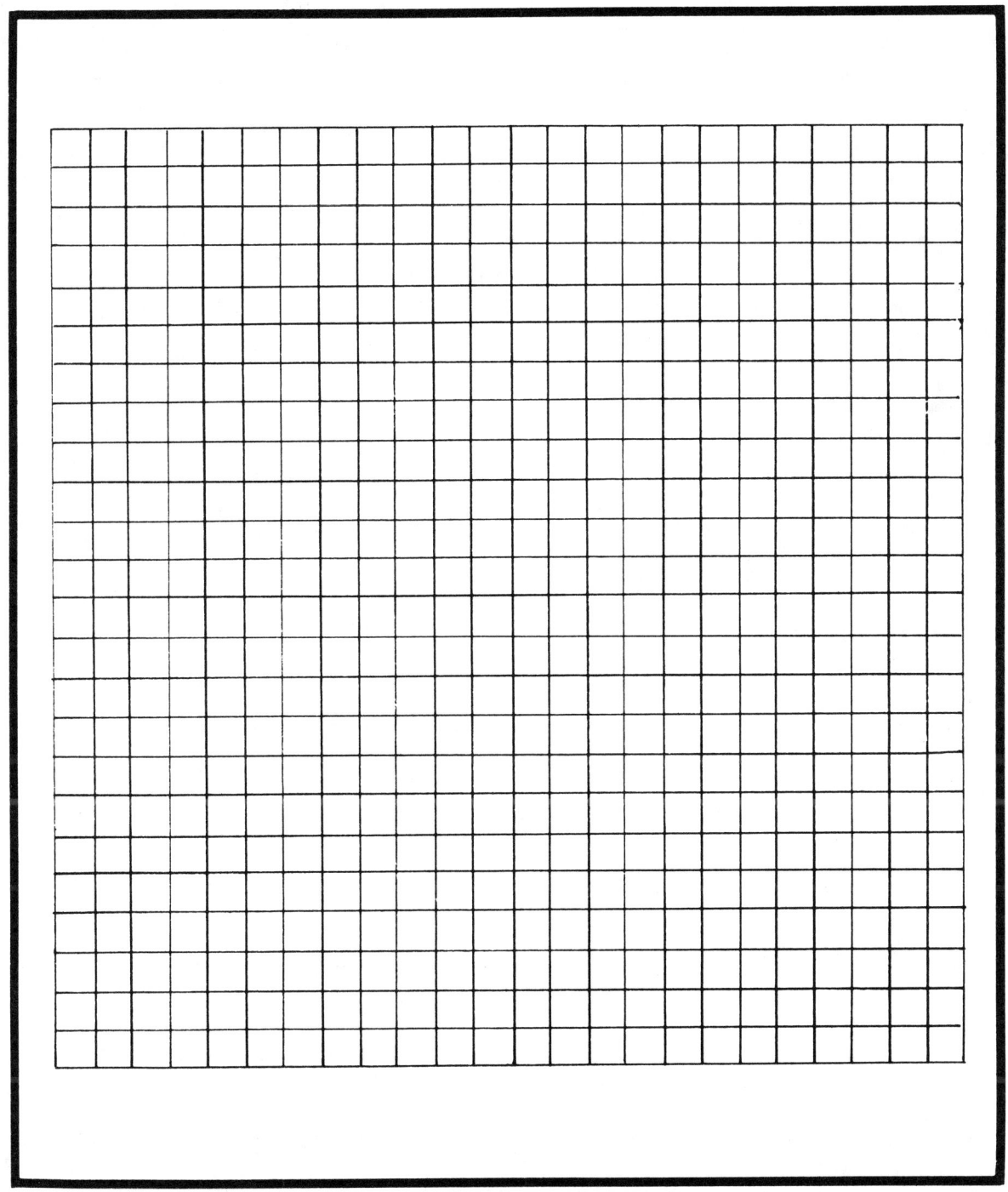

PLANT RECORDS

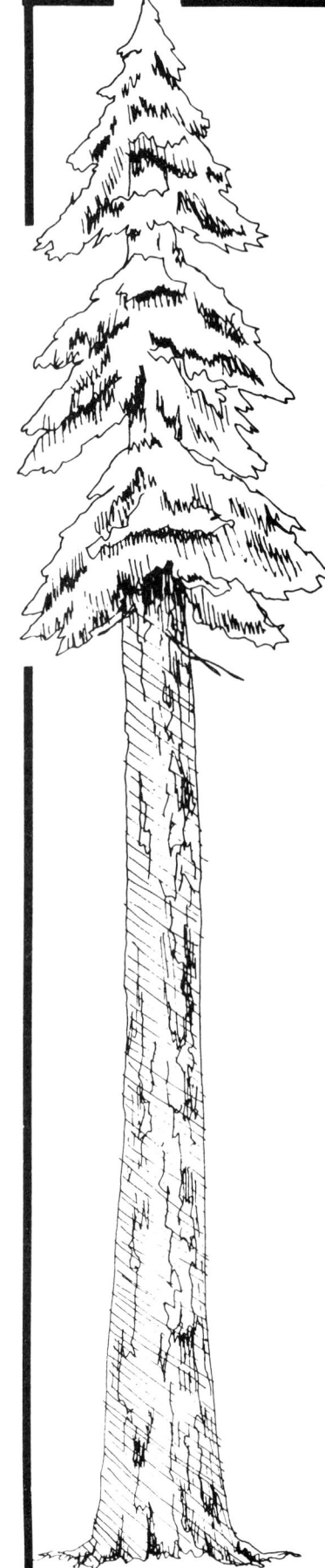

PURPOSE: To have students test their knowledge of various records held by plants.

MATERIALS: Matching exercise such as the following concerning the records held by various plants and reference books.

PROCEDURE: Use reference books to answer the matching exercise below.

Redwood tree	Coconut
Bristlecone pine tree	Amanita (death cup)
Orchid	Black ironwood tree
Ginkgo tree	Toothed grass
Duckweed	Wild fig tree

Do you know which of the above plants ....?

1. _____ is the plant most widely grown in the world.

2. _____ is the tallest plant in the world.

3. _____ is the oldest living plant.

4. _____ is the most ancient species of tree in the world.

5. _____ is the plant which bears the largest seed.

6. _____ is the plant with the heaviest (most dense) wood.

7. _____ is the plant with the largest roots.

8. _____ is the smallest flowering plant.

9. _____ is probably the most poisonous fungus.

10. _____ is the flowering plant with the smallest seeds.

MY SCIENCE PROGRESS

PURPOSE: To show improvement or the lack of it in science grades.

MATERIALS: Graph paper, pen or pencil.

PROCEDURE: Chart your grades to show your progress.

My Science Progress

Scores

100 100
95 95
90 90
85 85
80 80
75 75
70 70
65 65
60 60
55 55
50 50
45 45
40 40
35 35
30 30
25 25
20 20
15 15
10 10
5 5
0 0

Dates

ANSWER KEY

Page 1: Mobile Classification of Plants

Activity

Page 3: Tree Stem (These answers are for the illustration)

1. a. annual rings
   b. heartwood
   c. cambium
   d. sapwood
   e. bark
   f. rays
2. 18 years old
3. 1955
4. Heartwood
5. Sapwood
6. Heartwood
7. Heartwood
8. Young tree
9. No
10. Answers will vary
11. Answers will vary

Page 5: Story of a Tree

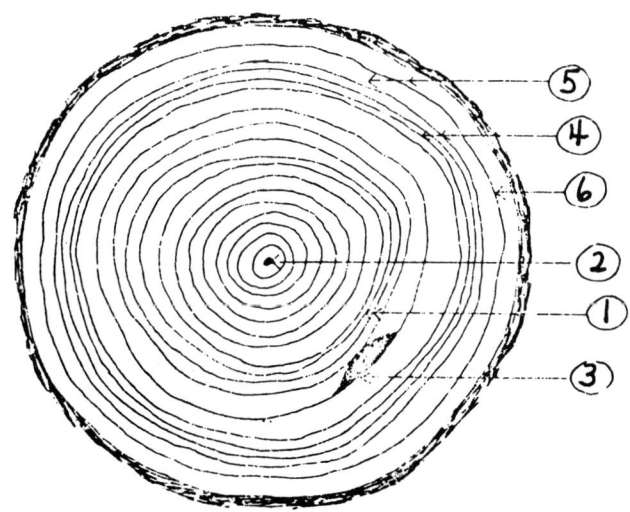

56

ANSWER KEY

Page 7: Parts of a Flower

    1. Anther
    2. Filament
    3. Stigma
    4. Petal
    5. Style
    6. Sepal
    7. Ovary

Page 8: Questions:

    1. Anther and filament
    2. Stigma, style, and ovary
    3. Ovary
    4. Anther
    5. Petals and sepal
    6. Bees or other insects. Insects are attracted to color and fragrance.
    7. No. The stigma is taller than the anther.
    8. Answers will vary.
    9. Staminate flowers contain only male reproductive parts.
  10. Pistillate flowers contain only the female parts.
  11. Answers will vary.
  12. Answers will vary.
  13. Answers will vary.

Page 10: What is Germination?

    1. 86
    2. 14
    3. 86%
    4. 14%
    5. Good soil, water, sunshine, etc.
    6. Water his garden; apply fertilizer.
    7. Yes
    8. Bad seeds, insects, too much rain, etc.
    9. Answers will vary
  10. Answers will vary

ANSWER KEY

Page 12: A Melon Explosion!

      1. 100
      2. 10,000
      3. 10,000,000
      4. There would be a population explosion of this plant.
      5. Drought, poor soil, overcrowding, insects, etc.
      6. The cod produces more eggs than can possibly survive; the melon produces more seeds than will survive.
      7. Very few eggs develop and survive into adult cod.
      8. Answers will vary.

Page 13: Transportation of Water in Celery

      Activity

Page 15: Problems of Classification

      Activity

Page 17: How to Use a Simple Key

      Activity. Solution given on Page 18

Page 21: A Tree Key

      a. Horse Chestnut
      b. Longleaf Pine
      c. Dogwood
      d. Black Spruce
      e. American Elm
      f. Black Walnut

Page 22: Biotic Field Trip

      Activity. Answers will vary.

Page 25: Making a Leaf Collection

      Activity

ANSWER KEY

Page 26: Tree Silhouettes

      1. Columnar - Lombardy Poplar
      2. Spreading - White Oak
      3. Vase - American Elm
      4. Weeping - Weeping Willow
      5. Oval - Sugar Maple

For other examples the answers will vary.

Page 28: Plant Drawings

Page 29: Monocot Germination

      1. Corn seed
      2. Embryo
      3. Plumule (first leaf)
      4. Cotyledon
      5. Radicle
      6. Leaf
      7. Lateral root (side root)
      8. Primary root (main root)

Page 30: Dicot Germination

      1. Radicle
      2. Bean seed
      3. Hypocotyl
      4. Primary root (main root)
      5. Seed Coat
      6. Plumule (first leaf)
      7. Leaf
      8. Cotyledons
      9. Lateral root (side root)
    10. Primary root (main root)

Page 31: Monocot Stem

      1. Rind
      2. Pith
      3. Phloem
      4. Xylem

ANSWER KEY

Page 31: Dicot Stem

   5. Cortex
   6. Phloem
   7. Cambium
   8. Pith
   9. Xylem

Page 32: Leaf Structures

   1. Palisade cell
   2. Epidermis
   3. Cuticle
   4. Palisade layer
   5. Spongy layer
   6. Lower epidermis
   7. Guard cells
   8. Vascular bundle (vein)
   9. Stoma

Page 33: Root Tip

   1. Vascular cylinder
   2. Root hair
   3. Cortex
   4. Epidermis
   5. Root cap

   X-Section

   1. Cortex
   2. Xylem
   3. Phloem
   4. Epidermis

Page 34: Rotation Seed Lab

   Activity

Page 36: Tree Dating - Nature's Calendar

   1. 1930
   2. 1947
   3. 9
   4. 1938
   5. 18
   6. 17
   7. 1938, 1946
   8. 1941, 1945, 1946, 1947, 1951, 1954

Page 38: Tree Calendars

   Activity

Page 39: Repeat a Famous Experiment of Robert Hooke

   Activity

ANSWER KEY

Page 40: Color Them Poisonous

                Activity

Page 45: Building a Sugar Molecule

1. Six molecules, 12 atoms
2. Red
3. Oxygen
4. Photosynthesis
5. $6CO2 + 6H20 = C6H1206 + 602$

6. Plants use carbon dioxide and water to make simple sugar and oxygen

Page 49: Tree Bingo

                Activity

Page 50: A Nature Field Trip

                Activity.   Answers will vary.

Page 53: Plant Records

1. Toothed grass
2. Redwood tree
3. Bristlecone pine
4. Ginkgo
5. Coconut
6. Black ironwood tree
7. Wild fig tree
8. Duckweed
9. Amanita
10. Orchid

Page 54: My Science Progress

                Answers will vary.